Practice Test #1

Practice Questions

Verbal Skills

1. Aptitude most nearly means
    a. talent
    b. test
    c. height
    d. disposition

2. Which word does *not* belong with the others?
    a. guitar
    b. drummer
    c. saxophone
    d. piano

3. Approximate means the *opposite* of
    a. inexact
    b. precise
    c. attempt
    d. estimate

4. Which word does *not* belong with the others?
    a. furniture
    b. table
    c. desk
    d. chair

5. Eileen left for the airport after Sara left. David left before Sara. David left after Eileen. If the first two statements are true, then the third is
    a. true
    b. false
    c. uncertain

6. Sniper is to aim as tightrope walker is to
    a. circus
    b. net
    c. balance
    d. fear

7. Endearment most nearly means
    a. suspicion
    b. affection
    c. venison
    d. imprisonment

8. Eminent means the *opposite* of
    a. disliked
    b. inevitable
    c. mental
    d. interior

9. Earl has fewer coins than June. Dean has fewer coins than Earl. June has more than Dean. If the first two statements are true, then the third is
    a. true
    b. false
    c. uncertain

10. Which word does *not* belong with the others?
    a. helmet
    b. shoulder pads
    c. football
    d. kneepads

11. Repulsive most nearly means
    a. attractive
    b. gravitational
    c. pulse
    d. disgusting

12. Pool is to water as library is to
    a. a librarian
    b. a student
    c. books
    d. computers

13. Dexterity means the *opposite* of
    a. awkwardness
    b. agility
    c. skill
    d. discord

14. Achilles ran half as far as the tortoise. The rabbit ran twice as far as Achilles. The tortoise and rabbit ran the same distance. If the first two statements are true, then the third is
    a. true
    b. false
    c. uncertain

15. Minute is to clock as day is to
    a. calendar
    b. ruler
    c. yardstick
    d. measurement

16. Which word does *not* belong with the others?
    a. laptop
    b. MP3 player
    c. cell phone
    d. electronics

17. Ineligible means the *opposite* of
    a. flexible
    b. legible
    c. allowed
    d. banned

18. Electricity is to outlet as water is to
    a. plumber
    b. ice
    c. pool
    d. faucet

19. Which word does *not* belong with the others?
    a. The Great Depression
    b. World War Two
    c. History
    d. The Civil War

20. Infinite is to short as bottomless is to
    a. pit
    b. deep
    c. fathom
    d. shallow

21. Cordial means the *opposite* of
    a. inhospitable
    b. sterile
    c. beloved
    d. entwined

22. Mindful means the *opposite* of
    a. inattentive
    b. explosive
    c. knowledgeable
    d. telepathic

23. Liable most nearly means
    a. irresponsible
    b. responsible
    c. unable
    d. ineligible

- 5 -

24. Principal is to school as governor is to
    a. president
    b. capitol
    c. state
    d. government

25. Joni arrived in the canyon after Cass. Jackson arrived before Joni. Cass arrived before Jackson. If the first two statements are true, then the third is
    a. true
    b. false
    c. uncertain

26. Which word does *not* belong with the others?
    a. dentist
    b. professional
    c. lawyer
    d. dermatologist

27. Bare most nearly means
    a. concealed
    b. uniformed
    c. revealed
    d. dressed

28. Charitable most nearly means
    a. stingy
    b. generous
    c. poor
    d. profitable

29. Which word does *not* belong with the others?
    a. pizza
    b. sausage
    c. pepperoni
    d. onions

30. The matinee had twice as many viewers as the early show. The late show had twice as many viewers as the matinee. The matinee had eleven viewers.
    a. true
    b. false
    c. uncertain

31. Inanimate most nearly means
    a. active
    b. cartoon
    c. motionless
    d. animal

32. Tasteful means the *opposite* of
    a. vulgar
    b. delicious
    c. elevated
    d. acute

33. Elongated means the *opposite* of
    a. extended
    b. expanded
    c. shortened
    d. rounded

34. Dictate most nearly means
    a. allow
    b. tell
    c. prevent
    d. ask

35. Dorine won more awards than Heather won at the competition. Alice won fewer awards than Dorine. Heather won fewer awards than Alice.   If the first two statements are true, then the third is
    a. true
    b. false
    c. uncertain

36. Coca Cola is to soft drink as Xerox is to
    a. paper
    b. office
    c. writing
    d. copier

37. Robust means the *opposite* of
    a. rotund
    b. distracted
    c. sickly
    d. animated

38. Which word does *not* belong with the others?
    a. quotation marks
    b. punctuation
    c. semicolon
    d. period

39. Scissors is to haircut as tractor is to
    a. farmer
    b. harvest
    c. soil
    d. corn fields

40. Mutiny most nearly means
    a. revolt
    b. measurement
    c. ship
    d. ammunition

41. Which word does *not* belong with the others?
    a. pickup truck
    b. tugboat
    c. railroad car
    d. eighteen-wheeler

42. Accidental means the *opposite* of
    a. artificial
    b. intentional
    c. chance
    d. unanticipated

43. Which word does *not* belong with the others?
    a. Indian
    b. Ocean
    c. Pacific
    d. Atlantic

44. The first day took forever compared to the third day. The third day seemed to take twice as long as the second day. The second day did not seem as long as the first day. If the first two statements are true, then the third statement is
    a. true
    b. false
    c. uncertain

45. Active means the *opposite* of
    a. electrical
    b. moving
    c. inert
    d. positive

46. Opaque most nearly means
    a. crystal
    b. clear
    c. dark
    d. memorial

47. Question mark is to punctuation as screwdriver is to
    a. mechanic
    b. screw
    c. wrench
    d. tool

48. Year is to month as foot is to
   a. inch
   b. yard
   c. meter
   d. mile

49. Which word does *not* belong with the others?
   a. small intestine
   b. kidney
   c. liver
   d. anatomy

50. Berate most nearly means
   a. payment
   b. scale
   c. time
   d. scold

51. The ferry takes more people to the island than the helicopter. The underground train also takes more people than the helicopter. The train takes as many people as the ferry. If the first two sentence are true, then the third is
   a. true
   b. false
   c. uncertain

52. Which word does *not* belong with the others?
   a. interstate
   b. asphalt
   c. highway
   d. avenue

53. Obligation most nearly means
   a. legal
   b. commitment
   c. connective
   d. decay

54. Which word does *not* belong with the others?
   a. elementary
   b. school
   c. junior high
   d. college

55. Homage most nearly means
   a. household
   b. image
   c. mockery
   d. tribute

56. Flounder most nearly means
    a. decay
    b. struggle
    c. grapple
    d. flourish

57. Which word does *not* belong with the others?
    a. cumulus
    b. cirrus
    c. clouds
    d. stratus

58. Denny has more trading cards than Barry. Barry has fewer cards than Steve. Steve has more than Denny. If the first two sentences are true, then the third one is
    a. true
    b. false
    c. uncertain

59. Which word does *not* belong with the others?
    a. Jupiter
    b. moon
    c. Earth
    d. Saturn

60. Which word does *not* belong with the others?
    a. footballs
    b. basketballs
    c. hockey pucks
    d. sporting gear

Reading Comprehension

Passage One: PARENTING STYLES

When a newborn cries throughout the night, parents can feel at a loss. If they turn to expert advice, they find that even experts disagree on the best solution. The two most popular techniques could not be more <u>contradictory</u>: One encourages parents to let the infant cry himself to sleep. The other encourages "<u>co-sleeping</u>," or letting the infant sleep in the parents' bed.

In the first technique, popularized by Dr. Richard Ferber, parents are encouraged to stick to a strict schedule and teach the infant to adapt. The infant sleeps in a separate room; if he cries, the parents should wait five minutes to check on him. The next time he cries, the parents wait ten minutes. The next time, they wait fifteen. Gradually, the theory goes, the child learns to get back to sleep on his own. This is often called the "cry it out" solution.

At the other end of the spectrum is "attachment parenting." This technique was developed by Dr. William Sears, who argues that the parents should be available to care for the infant if he cries. This technique helps the infant feel that he can rely on his parents to take care of him.

Both sides have their critics. Ferber's technique seems <u>callous</u> and uncaring to some, and Sears's technique seems unsympathetic to sleep-deprived parents. In the end, parents must rely on the only tried and true technique: trial and error.

1. The main purpose of this passage is:
    a. To inform readers of two options available to parents of newborns.
    b. To convince readers that the "cry it out" method is best.
    c. To convince readers that "attachment parenting" is best.
    d. To criticize both methods.

2. The meaning nearest to the word <u>co-sleeping</u> is:
    a. "cry it out"
    b. "attachment parenting"
    c. To sleep together
    d. To take turns sleeping

3. Which of the following statements can be inferred from the final sentence of the passage?
    a. Parents should do what their parents did.
    b. Parents should choose one method or the other.
    c. Parents should experiment with both methods.
    d. Parents should ignore both methods.

4. Which of the following approaches would be part of Dr. Ferber's approach?
    a. Teach the infant to get himself to sleep.
    b. Teach the infant that he can depend on the parent.
    c. Teach the infant to sleep on its back to reduce the risk of Sudden Infant Death Syndrome.
    d. Swaddle the infant tightly.

5. The word <u>contradictory</u>, as used in the passage, most nearly means,
   a. False
   b. Deceitful
   c. Conflicting
   d. Inexact

6. Which of the following actions would be in keeping with Dr. Sears's approach?
   a. Nurse the infant only at certain times of the day and night.
   b. Stay close to the infant and attend to his needs.
   c. Teach the child sign language so he can communicate from an early age.
   d. Reduce the amount of noise in the household.

7. The word <u>callous</u>, as used in the passage, most nearly means:
   a. Sensitive
   b. Insensitive
   c. Doting
   d. Flexible

8. Which of the following statements captures the main idea of the passage?
   a. Parents should sleep in shifts.
   b. Attachment parenting makes children more trusting.
   c. Both methods are wrong in different ways.
   d. Both methods have faults and strengths.

Passage Two: RECORDING TECHNOLOGY

Though a small number of purists maintain that records of the 1920s and 30s sound better,
    no one would argue that they sound more complex than those of the 21ˢᵗ Century.
    Recording technology has evolved into a very <u>intricate</u> process, and the end result
    often sounds as complex as the technology used to create it. There are three basic
    stages to the recording process: recording, mixing, and mastering.
Recording involves using microphones to capture the sound of instruments, but it can also
    involve software-based instruments. <u>Samples</u>, short recorded sounds triggered by a
    computer or keyboard, and synthesizers have come to replace real instruments in
    many recordings
In mixing, each sound from the recording is made to sound as clear as possible. The mixer
    will choose where to place the sound, either in the left or the right speaker, and
    whether to add certain textures to the sound, such as <u>reverb</u> or echo, which make
    some instruments sound further away than others. The mixer can also manipulate
    the recordings, for instance by making a vocal sound almost robotic.
The last stage, mastering, involves a process called EQ. This is done using a device similar to
    the treble and bass controls in a car stereo, but it is much more fine-tuned.
    Mastering can also make the recording louder. In all, modern recordings are highly
    complex and time-consuming to create, but the end result of this process yields rich
    sound experiences for the listener.

9. The author of this passage is attempting to:
    a. Persuade the reader that recording technology sounded better in the 1920s.
    b. Explain some of the complex processes involved in creating 21st Century recordings.
    c. Argue that the mixing stage is the most important stage in the recording process.
    d. Teach the reader how to record a song.

10. The word <u>intricate</u> most nearly means:
    a. Complex
    b. Technological
    c. Robotic
    d. Beautiful

11. According to the passage, which of the following statements is true?
    a. EQ is short for "equalization."
    b. Only a listener who understands all the stages of the recording process can tell the
       difference between recordings of the 1920s and today.
    c. To perform music well, all musicians have to learn how to record, mix, and master a
       recording.
    d. Changes in technology have greatly impacted the process of recording music.

12. Which of the following statements can be inferred from the last paragraph?
    a. Anyone who can work a car stereo can master a record.
    b. Mastering is the easiest of the three stages of making a record.
    c. EQ can be used to control treble.
    d. EQ can make a vocal sound robotic.

13. As used in this passage, the word <u>reverb</u> means:
    a. To record something twice
    b. Reverse
    c. Something that makes instruments sound far away
    d. Mixing

14. Which of the following can be inferred from paragraph two?
    a. Synthesizers do not sound the same as real instruments.
    b. Samples are found inside a microphone.
    c. Synthesizers use samples of real instruments.
    d. Acoustic guitars are not used in recordings anymore.

15. In this passage, the word <u>samples</u> most nearly refers to:
    a. Short recordings of sounds
    b. Synthesizers
    c. The bass frequencies controlled by an EQ
    d. Mixing

16. Which of these statements seems most true based on the passage?
    a. Instruments are played during the mixing stage.
    b. Synthesizers are used to master a recording.
    c. Samples are recorded after the mixing process.
    d. Microphones are most often used during the recording process.

Passage Three: CLOUD FORMATION

It is common knowledge that clouds are made of water, but how did the water get there? Why doesn't it fall? Why does the water appear white in its cloud form but not white when we see it on the ground? The knowledge necessary to answer these questions may not be so common after all.

How does it get there? The Sun's heat is the main cause. When it shines on water, the water evaporates and rises into the air in the form of vapor. This vapor is invisible until it reaches higher levels of the atmosphere, where the temperature is much colder. There the water vapor begins to cool down and turn back into tiny droplets of water. If you've ever seen the white <u>condensation</u> that rises above a pot of boiling water, then you've seen a cloud up close.

Why doesn't it fall? It would seem that the water would fall from the sky since it is common knowledge that water is heavier than air. One droplet of water from a cloud, however, is about 10,000 times smaller than a grain of salt. The <u>currents</u> of air in the atmosphere hold these tiny droplets up.

Why is this water white? When you shine a red, green, and yellow light together, they combine to form one white light. Likewise, when sunlight (which contains all the colors of the rainbow) passes through the tiny droplets in a cloud, it scatters all the different colors of light in every direction. It appears as the color white to us because we are seeing all the colors of the rainbow at the same time.

17. The word <u>condensation</u>, as used in this passage, most nearly means:
    a. Dry
    b. Steam
    c. Boiling
    d. Atmospheric pressure

18. Which of the following statements can be inferred from this passage?
    a. Water can take on different forms depending on the temperature.
    b. Clouds are an optical illusion.
    c. The effect of gravity's pull on water vapor makes clouds look white.
    d. Clouds are made of more than just water.

19. In this passage, the word <u>currents</u> most likely refers to:
    a. Electricity
    b. Tides
    c. Wind
    d. Vapor

20. Which of the following statements captures the main idea of the passage?
    a. Common knowledge is always wrong.
    b. White light is visible when all the colors of the rainbow are present.
    c. The properties of clouds are a result of physical causes.
    d. The water droplets in clouds are too small to fall.

21. Why does the first paragraph list all the questions the essay will go on to answer?
    a. They give a quick overview of the essay's organization.
    b. The readers are expected to answer the questions themselves.
    c. All good writing should start with questions.
    d. These questions form the thesis statement, which should always be phrased as a question.

22. Which of the following statements can be inferred from the third paragraph?
    a. Clouds do not fall from the sky because water is always lighter than air.
    b. A grain of salt will hang suspended on air currents.
    c. Gravity does not pull on objects of such a small size.
    d. For an object as small as the droplets in a cloud, air pressure is stronger than gravity.

23. According to the passage, which of the following statements is true?
    a. Clouds turn into rain when air currents disappear.
    b. Tiny droplets of water cause sunlight to scatter in every direction.
    c. Water is not white on the ground because sunlight cannot pass through it.
    d. Boiling water is the primary cause of air currents.

24. The author states that water vapor turns back into tiny droplets of water because:
    a. Sunlight is stronger at higher layers of the atmosphere.
    b. The cold temperature causes the water vapor to change form.
    c. Air currents cause the droplets of water to separate from the water vapor.
    d. When the water vapor scatters sunlight, it frees the tiny droplets of water.

Passage Four: ALCIBIADES

Alcibiades, born in Athens, Greece, around 450 B.C., was a man of great influence. As a child, he refused to play the flute because he thought it made him look unattractive, and the flute fell out of favor with Athenian youth. As an adult, when he argued that Athens should attack Sicily, the Athenians followed him into a disastrous battle.

Alcibiades switched <u>allegiances</u> several times during the war between Athens and Sparta. He betrayed Athens by forming an alliance with its enemies, the Spartans, whom he led to several successful battles against the Athenians. He was exiled from Sparta for having an inappropriate relationship with the wife of the king, and he went into exile in Persia, enemy of both Athens and Sparta. There Alcibiades allied himself with a local governor, or <u>satrap</u>, whom he helped plot against both Athens and Sparta. Eventually, the Athenians allowed him to return home, where he led several victories against the Spartans. After a defeat, however, Alcibiades was exiled again.

He fled to one of his castles on the coast, where by coincidence he had a view of both the Spartan and Athenian fleets. When he tried to warn the Athenians of the Spartans' superior position, he was ignored. The Athenians suffered a devastating defeat that gave Sparta the upper hand in the war.

According to one account, Alcibiades was murdered in 404 B.C. because he was living with a woman, and her brothers burned his house down to protect her honor. Another account claims that Alcibiades was killed by order of the king of Sparta.

25. What is the main topic of the first paragraph?
    a. Alcibiades' influence over his contemporaries
    b. Alcibiades' childhood
    c. Alcibiades' musicianship
    d. Alcibiades' role in the attack of Sicily

26. <u>Satrap</u> is a word meaning:
    a. A Greek warrior
    b. A Persian leader
    c. A traitor
    d. Someone from Sparta

27. Which is the true reason Alcibiades was murdered?
    a. He violated a code of honor in the community where he lived.
    b. He was seen as a threat to the Spartan leaders.
    c. We don't know; history has preserved conflicting accounts of his death.
    d. He was murdered because he was a traitor.

28. The word <u>allegiances</u> most nearly means:
    a. Loyalty
    b. Influence
    c. Adultery
    d. Inhabitants of the Allegheny Mountains

29. Which of the following statements accurately explains why Alcibiades fled to his castle on the coast?
    a. So he could see the Spartan and Athenian fleets.
    b. So he could spy on the satrap.
    c. Because he had been exiled from Athens.
    d. Because he wanted to be able to communicate with both Athens and Sparta.

30. What is the main purpose of this passage?
    a. To inform the reader about the life of Alcibiades and the war between Athens and Sparta.
    b. To persuade the reader that Alcibiades was a victim of conspiracies.
    c. To prove that Alcibiades used his relationship with Sparta and Persia to gather information for Athens.
    d. To prove that history is never a fully accurate account of the past.

31. The author says that Alcibiades "allied himself" with the Persian satrap, which most nearly means:
    a. He spied on him.
    b. He had an inappropriate relationship with his wife.
    c. He betrayed him.
    d. He became his friend and confidant.

32. Which statement best captures the main idea of this passage?
    a. Alcibiades offended the king of Sparta by having an affair with his wife.
    b. Alcibiades switched allegiances many times during the war.
    c. Alcibiades wanted to become king.
    d. The Athenians should have listened to Alcibiades when he warned them of the position of the Spartan fleets.

Passage Five: QUANTUM WEIRDNESS

Imagine trying to play a game of basketball in a world without cause and effect. You could throw the ball but you couldn't predict what would happen next. It might pass right through the backboard or disappear for a moment and reappear in the hands of the other team's point guard.

While such a world sounds unimaginably bizarre, the activity it describes is not altogether different from the activity <u>physicists</u> see when they look at particles on the "<u>subatomic</u> level"— the level of existence that is smaller than the <u>electrons</u>, protons, and neutrons that make up atoms. Physicists call this the "quantum realm" and what they discover down there is that particles come in and out of existence without any clear cause. An electron can materialize in one place and then in another, apparently without having to pass through the space in between.

Physicists who are excited by what goes on in the quantum realm are always looking for ways in which our world, the world of basketballs and human bodies, behaves similarly to the quantum world. Some have proposed that brain cells act like quantum particles and that a thought can resemble an uncaused event. Other physicists caution against getting too carried away. They have shown that large-scale objects cancel out quantum weirdness. In a basketball, there may be some weird quantum properties, but they are only detectable on a scale of about 10^{-34} meters. This is a very small number, having thirty-three zeroes between the decimal and the one.

Physicists have largely ruled out finding quantum behavior in objects larger than an electron, which is billions and billions of times smaller than a basketball.

33. What is the main purpose of this passage?
    a. To prove that the human brain shows weird quantum properties.
    b. To prove that all objects are made of atoms.
    c. To inform the reader of the unusual properties of atoms that physicists have discovered.
    d. To demonstrate the physics of a basketball game.

34. <u>Physicists</u> are scientists who study:
    a. Physics
    b. Physiology
    c. Subatomic particles
    d. Physical education

35. According to the third paragraph, the number 10^{-34} is best described as:
    a. A minuscule number
    b. An enormous number
    c. The number of molecules in a basketball
    d. The distance between a proton and an electron

36. Which of the following statements can be inferred from this passage?
    a. All physicists believe that basketballs can disappear.
    b. Some physicists have argued that brain cells cannot act like quantum particles.
    c. No physicists believe in cause and effect anymore.
    d. Some physicists deny the existence of subatomic particles.

37. The word <u>subatomic</u> most nearly refers to:
    a. The world found at the level of molecules.
    b. The cells that make up the human brain.
    c. The world smaller than the atom.
    d. The molecules that make up a basketball.

38. According to the passage, an <u>electron</u> is:
    a. A unit of measurement.
    b. An electrical cloud that surrounds a molecule.
    c. A subatomic particle.
    d. One of the elements listed on the periodic table.

39. Reread the first three sentences of paragraph 3. Which one of the following statements most closely captures the author's meaning in this sentence, "Other physicists caution against getting too carried away"?
    a. Some physicists think this interpretation goes too far.
    b. Some physicists think this interpretation is not creative enough.
    c. Some physicists think this interpretation is correct.
    d. Some physicists think others are lying in order to get attention.

40. It can be inferred from this passage that:
    a. All physicists agree about the meaning of quantum weirdness.
    b. Physicists don't know whether quantum weirdness is cancelled out in large objects.
    c. Physicists have observed that the quantum world and the visible world are very different.
    d. Physicists think that the quantum world is not real.

Reading Vocabulary Practice Questions

41. to <u>skulk</u> quietly
    a. sniff
    b. plan
    c. sneak
    d. talk

42. the <u>smoldering</u> warehouse
    a. reeking
    b. smoking
    c. empty
    d. enormous

43. the <u>mulish</u> employee
    a. stubborn
    b. predictable
    c. unshaven
    d. impractical

44. a <u>hypocritical</u> politician
    a. confident
    b. persuasive
    c. authoritative
    d. insincere

45. to shout with <u>jubilation</u>
    a. consequence
    b. elation
    c. anger
    d. volume

46. the <u>belated</u> gift
    a. beautiful
    b. overdue
    c. inexpensive
    d. sincere

47. to <u>monopolize</u> one's time
    a. dominate
    b. waste
    c. devote
    d. trade

48. his <u>faltering</u> defense
    a. hesitating
    b. proud
    c. decisive
    d. impractical

49. the <u>unanimous</u> decision
    a. difficult
    b. undisputed
    c. praised
    d. predictable

50. the <u>imminent</u> change
    a. royal
    b. painful
    c. unavoidable
    d. soon-to-occur

51. to <u>radiate</u> in every direction
    a. search
    b. shine
    c. travel
    d. strike

52. the <u>bountiful</u> dinner
    a. scarce
    b. inedible
    c. joyful
    d. plentiful

53. her <u>listless</u> mood
    a. lethargic
    b. scared
    c. hyperactive
    d. undetermined

54. our national <u>heritage</u>
    a. accent
    b. tradition
    c. pride
    d. income

55. to <u>compel</u> one's peers
    a. repay
    b. insult
    c. disgrace
    d. influence

56. a persistent cough
    a. ongoing
    b. loud
    c. hollow
    d. contagious

57. the <u>defaced</u> statues
   a. restored
   b. vandalized
   c. intricate
   d. prominent

58. the unpopular <u>tariff</u>
   a. official
   b. vote
   c. law
   d. tax

59. the disadvantaged child
   a. deprived
   b. victorious
   c. adopted
   d. gifted

60. a far-reaching <u>proclamation</u>
   a. announcement
   b. disease
   c. summons
   d. shockwave

61. an <u>artificial</u> ingredient
   a. natural
   b. synthetic
   c. toxic
   d. unnecessary

62. an indivisible <u>particle</u>
   a. large
   b. aquatic
   c. element
   d. whole

Language

Usage, Punctuation, and Grammar Practice Test

Select the sentence with an error in usage, punctuation, or grammar. If no errors are found, choose choice d.

1.
   a. Wind always blows from areas of higher to lower atmospheric pressure.
   b. Tillie, the German shepherd was always the first one to know when Dad got home.
   c. Throughout his testimonial, the witness cleaned his glasses with his tie.
   d. No mistake.

2.
   a. Though I had only met him recently, I felt as though I had long known Jon.
   b. There were very few people left on the streets after sundown.
   c. There are over 600 species of bacteria living in the human mouth at any time.
   d. No mistake.

3.
   a. The world's population, growing at 4.2 births every second and dropping by 1.7 deaths.
   b. Woodrow Wilson said, "You are here to enrich the world and you impoverish yourself if you forget that errand."
   c. The word "infant" originally meant "not speaking," and the word "nice" meant "ignorant."
   d. No mistake.

4.
   a. The highest point on Earth is 29,028 feet, at the top of Mt. Everest, and the lowest is 36,198 feet below sea level, in the Mariana Trench near the Philippines.
   b. The Guggenheim Museum in Manhattan was designed by renowned architect Frank Lloyd Wright.
   c. The great Aswan Dam was built in 1902 in Egypt to help farmers irrigate their crops and to prevent his fields from flooding.
   d. No mistake.

5.
   a. The Fourth of July fireworks display always upsets our neighbors' dogs.
   b. The field of Medical Geography studies the ways a disease spreads throughout a region, the field was created in 1854 when a physician mapped out all the cholera cases in London and connected many of them to a single contaminated water pump.
   c. The equinoxes take place on the 21st of March and September.
   d. No mistake.

6.
   a. The electrical outlet had a long charred trail above it.
   b. The coliseum in Rome was once quarried to supply raw materials for nearby churches.
   c. The children were instructed to hold hands until we arrived at the park.
   d. No mistake.

7.
   a. The governor wanted to legalize bottle rockets again to keep people from crossing state lines to purchase fireworks.
   b. When Sumo wrestlers lift their legs and stomp the floor, their movements reflect an ancient Shinto ritual for driving away demons.
   c. There is many healthy vegetables in my grandmother's garden.
   d. No mistake.

8.
   a. Studies show that adolescents who believe they will die before the age of 35 are more likely to engage in dangerous, risk-taking behavior.
   b. The Wardrops' estate had fallen into disrepair until they attracted the interest of the local historical preservation society.
   c. Students who try to remember their homework assignments instead of writing them down rarely remembers everything correctly.
   d. No mistake.

9.
   a. Some viruses are very slow-acting and stay embedded in their hosts' cells.
   b. Some argued that many people would be unprepared for the switch from analog to digital television signals.
   c. Solids, liquids, and gasses are not separate types of matter, but three separately stages, like ice, water, and vapor.
   d. No mistake.

10.
   a. Skunks are "crepuscular," meaning they are most active at twilight.
   b. Roy pasted glow-in-the-dark pictures of all nine planets in our solar system on his ceiling they turned green when he turned off the light.
   c. While he was emperor of Rome, Tiberius did not live there; instead, he lived on an island and sent his orders by lantern, using a code called "semaphore."
   d. No mistake.

11.
   a. Rachel named her new pet blowfish "Carl" because that was the name of the clerk who sold it to her at the pet store.
   b. In North Weymouth, Massachusetts, Pilgrim Congregational Church allows members to bring their pets to the church service.
   c. Pete was well known for his impersonations.
   d. No mistake.

12.
   a. Orange Pekoe is my favorite tea.
   b. Only two people showed up to the garage sale all day.
   c. Not one of the tomato plants survived the freeze.
   d. No mistake.

13.
   a. Norma included a handheld vacuum cleaner in the picnic basket.
   b. No one was injured when the car slipped out of gear and rolled downhill into the lake.
   c. No one were allowed in the restaurant until the police had left.
   d. No mistake.

14.
   a. The last time I went to Nevada, I get a terrible sunburn.
   b. Martin Waldseemueller is remembered for his publication of a map in 1507 that was the first to use the name "America."
   c. No one seemed readier to leave the ceremony than the guest of honor.
   d. No mistake.

15.
   a. Mediterranean fishermen kills an octopus by biting it behind each eye.
   b. Maurice and Robin Gibb, two of the members of the Bee Gees, are twin brothers.
   c. Fortunately, no one arrived in time to see the enormous mess I'd made in the kitchen.
   d. No mistake.

16.
   a. Many hotels throw out linens after they are a month old, some have started donating them to those in need.
   b. Luxembourg is only 51 miles from north to south and, at its widest, 35 miles across from east to west.
   c. Atoms combine with other atoms to form molecules.
   d. No mistake.

17.
   a. The United States is allowed to lease Guantanamo Bay from Cuba for a naval base as part of an agreement that dates back to 1902.
   b. The U.S. did not officially have time zones until Congress' passed the Standard Time Act of 1918.
   c. The stinging tentacles of anemones are called nematocysts.
   d. No mistake.

18.
   a. No one at the table even noticed that the man was choking until the waiter rushed over to perform the Heimlich maneuver on him.
   b. The committee members couldn't hardly conceal their enthusiasm for the new measure.
   c. Nero, Emperor of Rome, is believed to be responsible for a fire that burnt much of that city.
   d. No mistake.

19.
   a. Much whispering broke loose in the chapel when the groom appeared with a black eye.
   b. No one mentioned George's job loss during dinner.
   c. After Michael worked three shifts on Saturday and slept all day Sunday.
   d. No mistake.

20.
  a. L-Taurine is an amino acid that is said to help with depression.
  b. On the equinox, night and day is the same length.
  c. Joel should have secured the cage better because the dog got out of the kennel in mid-flight.
  d. No mistake.

21.
  a. Jesse finished the crossword puzzle in twenty minutes.
  b. It is unlikely that we will see much of the money from the settlement after the lawyers and court fees are paid.
  c. It is not correct to call people from Wales, Scotland, or Northern Ireland "English" because they are not from England, they are Welsh, Scottish, or Irish.
  d. No mistake.

22.
  a. It is estimated that one million people died during the potato famine in Ireland from 1845–1850, while another two million immigrated to other countries.
  b. Pete always mow the yard with a can of Raid wasp spray in his pocket.
  c. The jacket was nice, but the sleeves were too short.
  d. No mistake.

23.
  a. The radio station broke a record by playing "Stairway to Heaven" ninety times in a row.
  b. The pledge drive lasted a week.
  c. The post office clerk asked whether the heavy package I'd ordered contained rocks or dumb bells?
  d. No mistake.

24.
  a. The population of the U.S. rose by two million People in between 2008 and 2009, reaching 305,529,237.
  b. Scientists think that Christopher Columbus died from a bacterial infection that he caught from the parrots aboard his ship.
  c. Some corn crops create their own insecticides.
  d. No mistake.

25.
  a. Very little life can be found above 27,000 feet, and no animals are known to live below 35,800 feet below sea level.
  b. Saturn's rings are invisible when they face Earth edge-on because they are not thick enough to be seen through a telescope.
  c. The record for the world's lowest temperature is held by Siberia, where temperatures reached ninety degrees below zero on February 6 1933.
  d. No mistake.

26.
- a. William Bryant was the first african-American to serve as a federal judge.
- b. The so-called railroad worm glows red on its head and greenish-yellow along its eleven segments.
- c. In snow storms, cattle huddle so closely together that they are more likely to die of suffocation than freeze to death.
- d. No mistake.

27.
- a. Belgium, The Netherlands, and Luxemburg is known as the "low countries" because of their low elevation.
- b. The restaurant was sued for not being accessible to the handicapped.
- c. The North Magnetic Pole is moving at a rate of about 25 miles per year.
- d. No mistake.

28.
- a. In between performances, the musicians paced backstage on their cell phones.
- b. In 1582, Pope Gregory declared October 5 to be changed to October 15 to correct the calendar.
- c. I was not the first person to compliment Ira on his new glasses.
- d. No mistake.

29.
- a. I stood in line for the restroom for nearly fifteen minutes.
- b. Nebraska is the only state in the U.S. that doesn't have two legislative houses.
- c. Nate seemed uninterested in the celebration he was texting on his cell phone.
- d. No mistake.

30.
- a. In Native American societies that practice the "potlatch," individuals gain status by giving gifts.
- b. My grandfather went to the driving range the day after Christmas to try out the golf clubs we bought for him.
- c. I spent five hours trying to writes the speech I was supposed to give the next day.
- d. No mistake.

31.
- a. I drank the last of the milk from the refrigerator.
- b. The Hutterites' origins date back to the 16th Century in Europe.
- c. Hours after the football game ended, traffic remained backed up.
- d. No mistake.

32.
- a. Halfway to work, I realized I'd left my wallet at my House.
- b. The pressure of a gas rises as the temperature increases.
- c. Gertrude Stein once called Ezra Pound "the village explainer," and she added, "Very useful if you happen to be a village; if not, not."
- d. No mistake.

33.
    a. From the airplane, the two islands looked exactly like a lowercase "i."
    b. For a few days after the accident, I couldnt look from side to side.
    c. David Copperfield is widely considered to be Charles Dickens' best work.
    d. No mistake.

34.
    a. Few people seemed enthusiastic about the three-day bike tour after the weather hitted the triple digits.
    b. Except for a one-hundred mile stretch in Panama, the Pan-American Highway stretches all the way from Fairbanks, Alaska, to Buenos Aires, Argentina.
    c. Every year, Aunt Florence's Christmas fudge block arrived in the mail and had to be divided into equal chunks for each person in the family.
    d. No mistake.

35.
    a. Evan had a hard time getting back into his sleep schedule after school started.
    b. Eileen's poncho got caught in the elevator door.
    c. In downtown Enterprise, Alabama, one can find a monument in honor of the boll weevil.
    d. No mistake.

36.
    a. I had to wake Dorie to keep her from snoring during the ceremony.
    b. After eight hours on the airplane, all the infants onboard started crying.
    c. Elephants take mud baths to protect themselves against parasites sunburn and overheating.
    d. No mistake.

37.
    a. Angela earned three credits toward her high school diploma by doing extra credit work.
    b. Collin's uncle ran an after-school program called "Rock Climbers Rule," a name that Collin suggested.
    c. Christa's new cell phone had a laser pointer.
    d. No mistake.

38.
    a. Caves are formed when underground water comes into contact with a material it can dissolve, such as limestone.
    b. Carole researched the energy efficiency, of several brands of toaster.
    c. Beverly came in third place despite having the lead for most of the race.
    d. No mistake.

39.
    a. Mrs. Bellamy sang in a high Soprano voice that always stood out from the rest of the choir.
    b. Because he was too short, Cameron was not allowed on the roller coaster.
    c. Joseph Smith founded the Mormon religion after discovering gold plates buried in a hill near his home.
    d. No mistake.

40.
   a. Ashley's application for a student loan was denied, but she still planned to attend the university.
   b. Betsy packed her toothpaste toothbrush and dental floss in a plastic bag.
   c. Arteries carry more oxygen, and veins carry more carbon dioxide.
   d. No mistake.

41.
   a. An isotope of a hydrogen atom has the same number of protons as a regular hydrogen atom, but a different number of neutrons.
   b. Alice said, "I didn't invite him to the party in the first place."
   c. Alfred Hitchcock was a master at creating suspenseful films.
   d. No mistake.

42.
   a. After the crowd left, Everett picked up all the plates and cups.
   b. A radioactive element releases particles because its nucleus is not bound together in a stable way.
   c. Dolores asked whether I mights like to study piano with her.
   d. No mistake.

Spelling Practice Questions

Select the sentence with an error in spelling. If there are no errors, select answer choice "d".

43.
   a. The yellow flowers are daffodils, and the orange ones are tiger lilies.
   b. The bus arrived earlier then scheduled.
   c. After lightning struck the house, the television looked blurry.
   d. No mistake.

44.
   a. The black cat had one white side where it rubbed against the wet paint in the garrage.
   b. Mike shined his flashlight into the crawl space, and a centipede crawled out.
   c. The farmer had to go into the fields during the rain to shut off the irrigation system.
   d. No mistake.

45.
   a. The ambulance sirens in Europe sound two notes tuned to an interval called a "tritone."
   b. Grandmother was surprised to find that her two-year-old granddaughter had secretly packed an open tube of paint in her clean clothes.
   c. The word "piano" comes from the Italian word for "soft."
   d. No mistake.

46.
   a. The mellotron is an instrument that looks like a piano, but it uses prerecorded tapes of flutes and cellos instead of piano strings.
   b. Joel said the lasagna was as easy to eat as the soul of his shoe.
   c. Whenever it rains, doors are harder to close because the vapor in the atmosphere gets in the wood's pores and causes them to expand.
   d. No mistake.

47.
   a. Kudzu is an invasive vine that has overgrown seven million acres in the southeastern U.S.
   b. When an apple starts to decay, it releases a gas called ethylene, which can trigger decay in nearby apples.
   c. My father always asked me to hold his boot while he pulled his foot out.
   d. No mistake.

48.
   a. The camels at the zoo looked as though they were loosing their fur.
   b. Maltodextrin is a food additive that is used in artificial sweeteners for its sweet taste and in salad dressings as a thickening agent.
   c. Leo Fender, the creator of Fender guitars, was not a guitar player.
   d. No mistake.

49.
   a. When my jump rope broke, all of its tiny plastic pieces spilled all over the basketball court.
   b. Physicist Stephen Hawking suffers from a disease called ALS, better known as Lou Gehrig's disease.
   c. I thought my neice named her hamster after me, until she told me that there was an Uncle Richard in her favorite cartoon.
   d. No mistake.

50.
   a. The "stroopwafel" is a popular dessert in the Netherlands. It is made of two thin waffles held together by thick caramel syrup.
   b. The homework assignment took me all evenning to complete.
   c. I thought my bicycle was stolen until I remembered getting a ride home from school.
   d. No mistake.

Composition Practice Questions

51. Where should the following sentence be placed in the paragraph below?
   Examples of these problematic beliefs are statements such as, "Everyone should love me" and "I must never be wrong."

   1] Albert Ellis created Rational Emotive Behavioral Therapy in the 1950s. 2] His primary aim was to help people overcome the problematic beliefs that cause them unhappiness. 3] Ellis observed that most negative emotions are due to beliefs that come in the form of commands containing words like "should," "ought," or "must." 4] For instance, someone who is upset because a coworker complained about him to his boss could analyze his response and find that the source of the unpleasant emotion is the belief that "everyone must approve of me."
   a. After sentence 1
   b. After sentence 2
   c. After sentence 3
   d. After sentence 4

52. Where should the following sentence be placed in the paragraph below?
   Supporters of HFCS, however, point to research that shows no connection to obesity at all.

   1] High fructose corn syrup (HFCS) is a sweetener used in many foods and soft drinks. 2] HFCS is created by grinding corn into corn starch, processing the starch to turn it into corn syrup, and then treating it with enzymes to turn it into fructose. 3] The result is a cheap, very sweet syrup that shows up in many of the food and drinks we consume every day, particularly soft drinks. 4] Critics of HFCS cite research that seems to prove that it increases obesity. 5] Another controversy concerns the use of the phrase "natural ingredients" on products containing HFCS. 6] Supporters say that it can be called natural because it comes from corn, but critics argue that after all the processing it is put through, it is no longer appropriate to call it "natural."
   a. After sentence 1
   b. After sentence 2
   c. After sentence 3
   d. After sentence 4

53. Choose the word or words that best fill the blank.

     The members of the fraternity were accused of hazing the incoming freshmen, _____ none of the freshmen testified against them.

  a. but
  b. so
  c. because
  d. and

54. Choose the word or words that best fill the blank.

     "Detasseling," or sending groups of teenagers into corn fields to pluck the pollinating tassels from corn stalks, has become a rite of passage in many agricultural communities in the Midwest ____ for many teens, it is their first paying job.

  a. though,
  b. because,
  c. but,
  d. nonetheless,

55. Choose the word or words that best fill the blank.

     We felt proud that our garden produced zucchinis the size of an adult human leg, ___ we didn't realize they taste best when harvested early while still small.

  a. but
  b. instead
  c. nor
  d. while

56. Choose the sentence that is correct and most clearly written.
  a. Her five kittens under the back steps the gray cat hid.
  b. Under the back steps her five kittens were hidden by the gray cat.
  c. The gray cat hid her five kittens under the back steps.
  d. The five kittens were hidden under the back steps by the gray cat.

57. Choose the sentence that is correct and most clearly written.
  a. The kitchen was flooded by the broken pipe before the tiles starting to bulge.
  b. After the broken pipe flooded the kitchen, the tiles started to bulge.
  c. Before the tiles started to bulge, the kitchen is flooded by the broken pipe.
  d. The tiles started to bulge but not until after the kitchen was flooding by the broken pipe.

58. Choose the sentence that is correct and most clearly written.
  a. Jim bailed out the flooded basement by hand.
  b. By hand the flooded basement was bailing out by Jim.
  c. The flooded basement was bails out by hand by Jim.
  d. Bailed out by Jim by hand was the flooded basement.

59. Which sentence does *not* belong in the following paragraph?

1] There are many uses for recycled tires. 2] Industries can use them as a fuel source because they can burn for a long time. 3] Playgrounds can shred them and use them beneath jungle gyms to protect children if they should fall. 4] Accidents on playgrounds are far more common when there is no adult supervision. 5] Recycled tires can also be used by manufacturers of shoe soles and rubber boots.

a. Sentence 2
b. Sentence 3
c. Sentence 4
d. Sentence 5

60. Which sentence does *not* belong in the following paragraph?

1] "Alternative country," better known as "alt-country" has its roots in the music of Johnny Cash, Neil Young, and Bob Dylan, who combined country and rock music. 2] Bob Dylan's best work would have to be the albums *Blonde on Blonde* and *Highway 61 Revisited*. 3] Alt-Country can easily be distinguished from country music because it combines elements of other genres, such as rock and even experimental music. 4] Though artists like the Byrds and the Flying Burrito Brothers successfully combined country music with other genres of music in the 1960s and 1970s, alt-country was first labeled in the 1990s when bands like Uncle Tupelo and Whiskeytown started creating a new sound that sounded like country music, but it defied clear categorization.

a. Sentence 2
b. Sentence 3
c. Sentence 4
d. Sentence 5

Quantitative and Mathematics

Quantitative Skills

1. What number is six more than 1/3 of 90?
    a.   30
    b.   36
    c.   42
    d.   46

2. Which numeral comes next in the series: 116, 113, 107, 98, ...?
    a.   86
    b.   89
    c.   91
    d.   92

3. Examine (a), (b), and (c) and select the best answer.

    (a) $\dfrac{1}{5}$ of 30   (b) $\dfrac{1}{4}$ of 20   (c) $\dfrac{1}{3}$ of 15

    a.   (a) > (b) = (c)
    b.   (a) = (b) = (c)
    c.   (a) < (b) = (c)
    d.   (a) < (b) < (c)

4. If 12 inches = 1 foot, and 3 feet = 1 yard, how many inches are there in 2.5 yards?
    a.   86
    b.   90
    c.   94
    d.   96

5. Which of the following numbers yields an integer when divided by 13?
    a.   207
    b.   45
    c.   111
    d.   117

6. One third of what number is equal to 2 cubed?
    a.   16
    b.   20
    c.   24
    d.   27

7. The point A lies at the intersection of the diagonals of the square in the Figure. Examine the regions of the square and find the best answer.
    a.   I = II = III
    b.   I = II < III
    c.   I > II = III
    d.   I > II < III

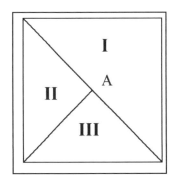

- 35 -

8. Evaluate 9 + 4(2 + 3)
    a. 20
    b. 22
    c. 24
    d. 29

9. Which of the following is NOT equivalent to the others?
    a. 0.24
    b. 24%
    c. $\dfrac{24}{10}$
    d. $\dfrac{12}{50}$

10. Evaluate 3 + [(12 ÷ 4)•6] – 20
    a. 1
    b. 6
    c. 8
    d. 0

11. What number subtracted from 45 makes three times 9?
    a. 27
    b. 21
    c. 18
    d. 16

12. Which numeral comes next in the series 54, 59, 63, 68, 72, …?
    a. 76
    b. 77
    c. 78
    d. 79

13. Which of the following lies between 1/3 and 2/3?
    a. 0.25
    b. 0.30
    c. 0.45
    d. 0.75

14. There are 12 inches in a foot. Which of the following is equivalent to 3 feet 4 inches?

    a. $3\frac{1}{2}$ feet

    b. $3\frac{1}{6}$ feet

    c. $3\frac{3}{4}$ feet

    d. $3\frac{1}{3}$ feet

15. Which numeral should fill in the blank in the series 2, 4, 8, ___, 32, 64?
    a. 12
    b. 16
    c. 20
    d. 24

16. Examine the isosceles triangle in the figure below and select the best answer choice.
    a. Angle A ≅ Angle B ≅ Angle C
    b. Angle A ≅ Angle B
    c. Angle B ≅ Angle C
    d. Angle A ≅ Angle C

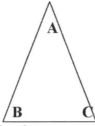

17. Which of the following numbers is a multiple of 23?
    a. 39
    b. 48
    c. 101
    d. 92

18. Which of the following is NOT a prime number?
    a. 76
    b. 17
    c. 41
    d. 23

19. Which number added to itself is 1/3 of 66?
    a. 22
    b. 11
    c. 33
    d. 44

20. Which numeral comes next in the series 3, 9, 27, 81, ...?
    a. 48
    b. 54
    c. 64
    d. 72

21. Which of the following is the greatest?
    a. 6 – 2
    b. -4 – 2
    c. -4 – (-10)
    d. 11 – 6

22. What number is one half the average of 7, 14, 22, and 23?
    a. 8.25
    b. 9.
    c. 9.25
    d. 16.5

23. Examine the Figure below, in which $AB = BC$, and select the best choice.
    a. The area of the rectangle equals that of the triangle
    b. The area of the rectangle is twice that of the triangle
    c. The area of the rectangle is half that of the triangle
    d. The area of the rectangle is more than twice that of the triangle

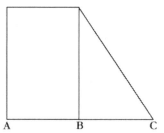

24. An odd number is multiplied by an even number, and the result is multiplied by another odd number. The final result must be
    a. Odd
    b. Even
    c. Negative
    d. Positive

25. A number less than zero is multiplied by a negative number. The result must be
    a. Odd
    b. Even
    c. Positive
    d. Negative

26. Which number should fill in the blank in the series 18, 23, 27, __, 32, 33?
    a. 28
    b. 29
    c. 30
    d. 31

27. Which of the following expressions is equal to 4(6 + 1)?

a. $\dfrac{100}{4}$

b. $\dfrac{100}{2}$

c. $\dfrac{28}{2}$

d. $\dfrac{56}{2}$

28. The product of two prime numbers must be
a. prime
b. odd
c. not prime
d. negative

29. A positive integer is subtracted from a smaller positive integer. The result must be
a. Odd
b. Even
c. Positive
d. Negative

30. Evaluate (3 + 1)(6 – 3)
a. 1
b. 12
c. 21
d. 15

31. In the Figure below, AB = CD and AC = BD. Find the best answer concerning the measures of angles ∠A, ∠B, ∠C, and ∠D.

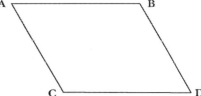

a. m∠A = m∠B and m∠C = m∠D
b. m∠A = m∠C and m∠B = m∠D
c. m∠A = m∠D and m∠B = m∠C
d. m∠A = m∠B = m∠C = m∠D

32. Which number is three times the difference between 17 and 36?
a. 57
b. 19
c. 38
d. 60

33. What number multiplied by 8 is 5 more than 59?
    a. 6
    b. 7
    c. 8
    d. 9

34. Examine (a), (b), and (c) and select the best answer.
    (a) 4^3 (b) 5^2 (c) 3^4
    a. $a > b > c$
    b. $a > b < c$
    c. $a < b < c$
    d. $a < b > c$

35. Which number should come next in the series 7, 14, 28, 56, ___?
    a. 122
    b. 112
    c. 102
    d. 84

36. What number divided by 2 is $\dfrac{2}{3}$ of 66?
    a. 11
    b. 33
    c. 44
    d. 88

37. Examine (a), (b), and (c) and select the best answer.
    (a) 30% of 90   (b) 10% of 270   (c) 60% of 45
    a. $a < b < c$
    b. $a < b = c$
    c. $a = b < c$
    d. $a = b = c$

38. What number is half of the product of 4, 5, and 6?
    a. 40
    b. 50
    c. 60
    d. 80

39. Which of the following numbers lies between $\frac{2}{3}$ and $\frac{3}{4}$?

   a. $\frac{5}{6}$

   b. $\frac{9}{12}$

   c. $\frac{17}{24}$

   d. $\frac{12}{13}$

40. Which fraction is halfway between $\frac{2}{9}$ and $\frac{5}{9}$?

   a. $\frac{3}{9}$

   b. $\frac{5}{18}$

   c. $\frac{4}{9}$

   d. $\frac{7}{18}$

41. Which number should come next in the series -9, -6, -3, 0, __?
   a. 3
   b. 9
   c. 6
   d. -3

42. Examine the intersecting line segments in the figure. A, B, C, and D are the measures of the angles. Select the true statement.
   a. A = B and C = D
   b. A = C and B = C
   c. A = C and B = D
   d. A = D and B = C

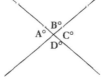

43. Examine (a), (b), and (c) and select the best answer.
   (a) 4(7 × 8)   (b) (4 × 7) × 8   (c) 4 × 7 × 8
   a. a = b = c
   b. a = b ≠ c
   c. a ≠ b = c
   d. a ≠ b ≠ c

44. The sum of 34 and what number is equal to the product of 7 and 6?
    a. 1
    b. 4
    c. 8
    d. 12

45. What number is 125% of 20?
    a. 30
    b. 34
    c. 22
    d. 25

46. Half of what number is equal to 15% of 70?
    a. 20
    b. 21
    c. 22
    d. 23

47. Which number should come next in the series 2011, 1999, 1987, 1975, __?
    a. 1968
    b. 1963
    c. 1959
    d. 1969

48. Examine (a), (b), and (c) and select the best answer.
        (a) an integer greater than 4 but less than 6
        (b) an integer equal to half of 10
        (c) a prime number greater than 3 but less than 7
    a. (a) must be equal to (b), but is not necessarily equal to (c).
    b. (a) must be equal to both (b) and (c).
    c. (a) is not necessarily equal to (b), but (b) must be equal to (c).
    d. None of the items is necessarily equal to any of the others.

49. Half of what number, multiplied by 3, equals the average of 10, 12, and 14?
    a. 6
    b. 7
    c. 8
    d. 10

50. Examine (a), (b), and (c) and select the best answer.

        (a) 90%   (b) $\dfrac{1}{9}$ (c) 0.9

    a. $a = b = c$
    b. $a = b \neq c$
    c. $a \neq b = c$
    d. $a \neq b \neq c$

51. The product of two even numbers must be
    a. a prime number
    b. an odd number
    c. a fraction
    d. an even number

52. Examine (a), (b), and (c) and select the best answer.
    (a) 0.8×0.7 (b) 0.08×0.07 (c) 0.008×0.007
    a. $a > b > c$
    b. $a < b < c$
    c. $a = b = c$
    d. $a > b < c$

Mathematics

1. Which of the following numbers is equal to 0.20?

   a. $\dfrac{1}{20}$

   b. $\dfrac{2}{100}$

   c. $\dfrac{1}{5}$

   d. $\dfrac{20}{1000}$

2. Which of the following numbers can be divided by 6 without a remainder?

   a. 34
   b. 18
   c. 22
   d. 93

3. Which of the following expressions is not a real number?

   a. $\dfrac{1}{5}$

   b. $\sqrt{17}$

   c. π

   d. $\dfrac{3}{0}$

4. Which of the following numbers is a prime factor of the number 121?

   a. 11
   b. 12
   c. 13
   d. 8

5. How much is 4.171 + 4.55 if the sum is rounded to the nearest tenth?

   a. 8.8
   b. 8.7
   c. 8.72
   d. 8

6. Which of the following rules describes the sequence 5, 25, 125, 625, ...?

   a. Multiply the position number by 5.
   b. Raise 5 to a power equal to the position number.
   c. Multiply 5 by the square of the position number.
   d. Add the product of 5 and the position number to 5.

7. Which of the following numbers is equal to 3^0?
   a. 0
   b. 1
   c. 3
   d. The number is not defined

8. Which of the following numbers is greatest?
   a. $\dfrac{1}{3}$
   b. $\dfrac{10}{33}$
   c. $\dfrac{100}{333}$
   d. $\dfrac{100}{330}$

9. Ray and his brother win a prize and share it equally. If each receives $15, what was the amount of the prize?
   a. $15
   b. $20
   c. $30
   d. $40

10. What is the area of a square with perimeter 44 cm?
    a. 16 cm²
    b. 11 cm²
    c. 1936 cm²
    d. 121 cm²

11. Sandra needs $3 more to buy a $12 book. How much money does she already have?
    a. $10
    b. $9
    c. $8
    d. $7

12. In the figure below, line segment AC bisects ∠BAD. If the measure of ∠BAC is 15°, what is the measure of ∠BAD?
    a. 45°
    b. 30°
    c. 20°
    d. 15°

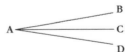

13. The graph below shows the average temperatures for each month during the year in the city of

Los Amares. During which period does the average temperature decrease by the greatest amount?
   a. December to January
   b. August to September
   c. March to April
   d. October to November

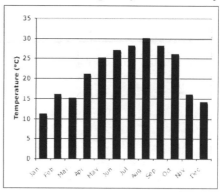

14. Which of the following is the product of $(x - y)$ and -1?
   a. $(y - x)$
   b. $-(x + y)$
   c. $(-y - x)$
   d. $-(y - x)$

15. Which of the following represents the value of the "5" in 452?
   a. 5×1
   b. 5×10
   c. 5×2
   d. 5×0.1

16. In the Figure below, the coordinates of the point A are:
   a. (3,3)
   b. (3,2)
   c. (-2,-3)
   d. (2,3)

17. Add $2y + 3x + 11$ and $3x - y + 4$
   a. $y - 2x + 15$
   b. $y + 6x + 15$
   c. $y - 6x + 15$
   d. $6xy + 15$

18. Simplify the expression $4\dfrac{2}{3} + 7\dfrac{1}{5}$.

   a. $11\dfrac{3}{8}$

   b. $11\dfrac{3}{15}$

   c. $11\dfrac{13}{15}$

   d. $11\dfrac{4}{10}$

- 46 -

19. Which of the following has the longest perimeter?
    a. A square with sides 3 cm long
    b. A circle with a radius of 3 cm
    c. A rectangle with width of 1cm and length of 4 cm
    d. An equilateral triangle with sides 3 cm long

20. There are 16 ounces in a pound. If one apple weighs 6 ounces, what is the weight of 12 apples?
    a. 12 pounds
    b. 6 pounds
    c. 6 pounds 6 ounces
    d. 4 pounds 8 ounces

21. The ratio of cats to dogs at an animal shelter is 3:2. If there are 45 cats in the shelter, how many dogs are there?
    a. 30
    b. 2
    c. 32
    d. 40

22. Which of the following numbers is equal to 0.00512?
    a. 5.12×103
    b. 5.12×10^{-3}
    c. 51.2×10^{-3}
    d. 512×10^{-4}

23. Which of the following numbers is closest to -3?
    a. -3.15
    b. -3.1
    c. -2.95
    d. 3.005

24. Two odd integers, one positive and one negative, are multiplied. Choose the best answer below.
    a. The product must be odd and positive.
    b. The product must be even and negative.
    c. The product must be odd and negative.
    d. The product must be even and positive.

Problem Solving Practice Questions

25. What percentage of a 5-person basketball team is made up of 2 players?
    a. 30%
    b. 25%
    c. 15%
    d. 40%

26. A rectangle is 3.4 inches wide by 5.7 inches long. What is the area in square inches?
    a. 18.2
    b. 16.8
    c. 19.38
    d. 17.28

27. Tom deposits $3800 dollars in a savings account that pays 7% interest annually. How much does he have after one year?
    a. $4110.55
    b. $4052.70
    c. $4075.13
    d. $4066.00

28. Two men working full time can paint a room in 8 hours. How long will it take to paint the room if 5 men work at it full time at the same rate?
    a. 3 hours 24 minutes
    b. 3 hours 30 minutes
    c. 2 hours 54 minutes
    d. 3 hours 12 minutes

29. If N represents any number, which of the following is not equivalent to the others?
    a. 0.2N
    b. 20 N
    c. $\frac{1}{5}N$
    d. 20% of N

30. Brain tumors are diagnosed at a rate of 12 per 100,000 people per year. Cell phone users have been shown to be 240% as likely to have a brain tumor as others. How many brain tumors per 100,000 cell phone users are expected annually?
    a. 240
    b. 24.4
    c. 30.6
    d. 28.8

31. The temperature is 70°F at noon and is expected to rise by 4°F each hour during the afternoon. Which of the following equations might be used to determine H, the number of hours before the temperature reaches 86°F?

   a. $86 = 70 + 4H$
   b. $86 = 4 + 70H$
   c. $86 = (4 + 70)H$
   d. $86 = 4 + 70H$

32. In the figure below, a circle is inscribed within a square. If the circle has a radius equal to R, which of the following expressions describes the shaded area?

   a. a. $\pi R^2 - 4R$
   b. b. $R^2 - 4\pi$
   c. $R^2(4 - \pi)$
   d. $4R - \pi R^2$

33. What is the value of $3x^2 + 2y$ when $x = 3$ and $y = 7$?

   a. 10
   b. 16
   c. 41
   d. 34

34. $\dfrac{\sqrt{40}}{\sqrt{2}} =$

   a. $\sqrt{20}$
   b. $2\sqrt{20}$
   c. $2\sqrt{10}$
   d. $4\sqrt{10}$

35. When three consecutive integers are added together, the total is 123. What is the value of the first integer?

   a. 39
   b. 40
   c. 41
   d. 42

36. Three coins are tossed. What is the probability of the result being 3 heads?

   a. 1 chance in 4
   b. 1 chance in 6
   c. 1 chance in 8
   d. 1 chance in 16

37. In the figure below, line segments AB and CD are parallel and are intersected by a third line. If α = 135°, what is the measure of δ?
    a. 135°
    b. 45°
    c. 30°
    d. 35°

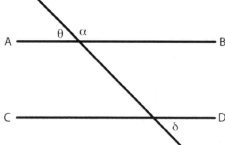

38. A point on the outer edge of a CD rotating at 500 RPM moves at a linear speed of 470 cm/s. What is the linear speed of a point halfway between the center and the outer edge of the CD?
    a. 117.5 cm/s
    b. 235 cm/s
    c. 470 cm/s
    d. 87.5 cm/s

39. Rafael drives at an average speed of 36 mph on a trip that lasts 2.5 hours. How far does he travel?
    a. 72 miles
    b. 80 miles
    c. 84 miles
    d. 90 miles

40. A courier service maintains a fleet of 60 vehicles. Three fifths of the vehicles are trucks, and the remainders are compact cars. In order to save on fuel costs, the service plans to replace half of the compact cars with hybrid vehicles. How many hybrids will they buy?
    a. 24
    b. 12
    c. 6
    d. 3

41. Kevin has 2 blue shirts, 6 black shirts, and 4 red shirts, which he keeps in the same drawer of his dresser. If he selects a shirt at random, what is the probability that it will be red or blue?
    a. 25%
    b. 50%
    c. 60%
    d. 65%

42. Andrea puts 10% of her paycheck into a savings account every week. At the end of a year (52 weeks), she has $1560 in her account. Assuming no interest has been paid, what is the amount of her weekly paycheck?
    a. $30
    b. $120
    c. $300
    d. $360

43. The table below shows Samantha's bowling scores during the month of April. What was her average score?

Game	1	2	3	4
Score	83	88	92	93

   a. 83
   b. 93
   c. 88
   d. 89

44. What is the area of the triangle shown in the Figure below?
   a. 16 square units
   b. 24 square units
   c. 10 square units
   d. 8 square units

45. The average of 6, 8, and x is equal to the average of x and 12. What is the value of x?
   a. 12
   b. 4
   c. -8
   d. -4

46. Given that $3(4x + 3) = 45$, what is the value of x?
   a. 2
   b. 3
   c. 4
   d. 5

47. $(44 + 3^2) + 2^2 = ?$
   a. 48
   b. 54
   c. 57
   d. 60

48. Consider two equal circles of radius r, as shown in the figure below. If B is the center of the first circle, and C is the center of the second circle, what is the length of line segment AD?
   a. 2r
   b. 3r
   c. 4r
   d. 2.5r

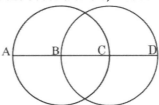

49. Charlotte's average score on 3 math tests was 86. After taking a fourth math test, her average for all four tests was 88. What was Charlotte's score on the fourth test?
   a. 94
   b. 93
   c. 92
   d. 91

50. Quentin buys a computer game that has been marked down by $25. He pays 80% of the normal price. What was the normal price of the computer game, before the mark down?
    a. $75
    b. $100
    c. $125
    d. $160

51. $\sqrt{40} = ?$

    a. $2\sqrt{2}\sqrt{5}$
    b. 20
    c. 5
    d. $4\sqrt{5}$

52. How many prime factors does the number 93 have?
    a. 2
    b. 3
    c. 4
    d. 5

53. $\dfrac{72}{17} = ?$

    a. $4 + \dfrac{3}{17}$

    b. $4 + \dfrac{1}{3 + \dfrac{1}{4}}$

    c. $4 + \dfrac{1}{4 + \dfrac{1}{4}}$

    d. $4 + \dfrac{1}{1 + \dfrac{1}{4}}$

54. Find the value of q if $\dfrac{q}{-16} = -64$.
    a. 1024
    b. -1024
    c. 4
    d. -4

55. Evaluate 15 + (16 – [2(11 – 6)] – 3)
    a. 15
    b. 18
    c. 28
    d. 30

56. In the figure below, the radius r of the circle is equal to 4 ft. The rectangle shown is a square. What is the shaded area?
    a. $16 – 4\pi$ ft²
    b. $64 – 4\pi$ ft²
    c. $16\pi – 8$ ft²
    d. $8 (8 – \pi)$ ft²

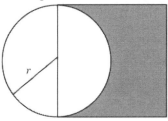

57. Find the value of x if $x^2 = \dfrac{81}{4}$.
    a. $\dfrac{3}{2}$
    b. $\dfrac{9}{4}$
    c. $\dfrac{9}{2}$
    d. $\dfrac{\sqrt{9}}{2}$

58. The perimeter of a square is 160 m. What is the area?
    a. 400 m²
    b. 1200 m²
    c. 1400 m²
    d. 1600 m²

59. If x + y = 17 and $\dfrac{1}{x} = 0.25$, what is the value of y?
    a. 68
    b. 34
    c. 17
    d. 13

60. If m2 = 9, which of the following could be a value of m?
    a. 4
    b. 6
    c. -3
    d. -2

61. A new candle is 21 cm high and burns at a rate of 3 cm per hour. When the candle is 9 cm high, how long has it been burning?
    a. 3 hours
    b. 3.5 hours
    c. 4 hours
    d. 4.5 hours

62. Gabriel buys a $22 book from a mail order firm. He must also pay a 10% tax and an additional $4 for shipping. What is his total cost for the book?
    a. $28.20
    b. $27.20
    c. $26.20
    d. $24.20

63. If $4^x = 256$, what is the value of x?
    a. 3
    b. 4
    c. 5
    d. 6

64. Pamela has 5 dollars more than one-third the dollars that Monica has. Which expression represents the amount of money that Pamela has?
    a. $5 + \dfrac{3}{m}$
    b. $5 + \dfrac{m}{3}$
    c. $\dfrac{5 \times 3}{m}$
    d. $5 - \dfrac{m}{3}$

Answers and Explanations

Verbal Skills

1. A: Aptitude means talent.

2. B: Drummer is the only word in the list that refers to a human being. The rest refer to musical instruments.

3. B: Approximate means estimated, the opposite of precise.

4. A: Furniture is the general class that all the other words in this group fit into.

5. B: We can diagram this as sequence follows: D > S > E. If it is true that David left for the airport before Sara, then he was the first of the three to leave. The third statement cannot be true.

6. C: A sniper must have good aim; a tightrope walker must have good balance.

7. B: Endearment most nearly means affection.

8. A: Eminent means esteemed or distinguished, the opposite of disliked.

9. A: We can diagram this account as follows: D < E < J. If June has more than Earl, and Earl has more than Dean, then June must have more than Dean.

10. C: Football is the only item in the list that a football player cannot wear.

11. D: Repulsive most nearly means disgusting.

12. C: A pool holds water; a library holds books.

13. A: Dexterity means agility, the opposite of awkwardness.

14. A: We can diagram this sequence as follows: A < T, A < R, T = R. If Achilles ran half the distance the tortoise ran, and the rabbit ran twice the distance of Achilles, the tortoise and the rabbit both ran the same distance.

15. A: Minutes are counted on a watch; days are counted on a calendar.

16. D: Electronics is the general class to which each of the other items in the list belongs.

17. C: Ineligible means disqualified, the opposite of allowed.

18. D: Electricity comes out of an outlet; water comes out of a faucet.

19. C: History is the general category to which all the other items in this list belong.

20. D: Infinite is the opposite of short; bottomless is the opposite of shallow.

21. A: Cordial means warm and friendly, the opposite of inhospitable.

22. A: Mindful means thoughtful, the opposite of inattentive.

23. B: Liable most nearly means responsible.

24. C: A principal is the main authority at a school; a governor is the main authority of a state.

25. C: We can diagram this sequence as follows: Cass < Joni, Jackson < Joni. The relationship between Cass and Jackson is not specified, so the third statement is uncertain.

26. B: Professional is the general category to which the other items in the list belong.

27. C: Bare most nearly means revealed.

28. B: Charitable most nearly means generous.

29. A: sausage, pepperoni, and onion are all ingredients of a pizza.

30. C: There is not enough information to determine the specific number of viewers, so the third statement is uncertain.

31. C: Inanimate most nearly means motionless.

32. A: Tasteful means refined, the opposite of vulgar.

33. C: Elongated means extended, the opposite of short.

34. B: Dictate most nearly means tell.

35. C: We can diagram this account as follows: H < D, A < D. The relationship between Heather and Alice is not specified, so the third statement is uncertain.

36. D: Coca Cola is a brand of soft drink; Xerox is a brand of copier.

37. C: Robust means healthy and vigorous, the opposite of sickly.

38. B: Punctuation is the general class to which the other items in the list belong.

39. B: Scissors are tools necessary for a haircut; a tractor is a tool necessary for harvest.

40. A: Mutiny most nearly means revolt.

41. B: Each item except for tugboat runs on land.

42. B: Accidental means unintentional, the opposite of intentional.

43. B: Ocean is the general category which contains all the other items in the list.

44. A: We can diagram this problem as follows: 1 > 3 > 2. The second day would seem shorter than the first because we know that it seemed shorter than the third, and that the first day was even longer than that.

45. C: Active means energetic and lively, the opposite of inert.

46. C: Opaque most nearly means dark.

47. D: A question mark is an example of punctuation; a screwdriver is an example of a tool.

48. A: A year contains months; a foot contains inches.

49. D: Small intestine, kidney, and liver are all examples of anatomy.

50. D: Berate most nearly means scold.

51. C: We can diagram this problem as follows: H < F, H < UT. Though we know that both the train and ferry take more people than the helicopter, we don't have enough information to know if they take the same number of people.

52. B: Interstate, highway, and avenue are all types of road. Asphalt is used in road construction, but is not a type of road.

53. B: Obligation most nearly means commitment.

54. B: School is the general class to which the other items belong.

55. D: Homage most nearly means tribute.

56. B: Flounder most nearly means struggle.

57. C: Cumulous, cirrus, and stratus are all types of clouds.

58. C: We can diagram this problem as follows: B < D, B < S. The problem does not give enough information to determine whether Steve has more than Denny.

59. B: Jupiter, Earth, and Saturn are planets that orbit the sun; the moon orbits the Earth.

60. D: Footballs, basketballs, and hockey pucks are all examples of sporting gear.

Reading Comprehension

1. **A:** Since the passage does not promote one view over the other, Answers B and C are incorrect. Whereas the passage does criticize both methods, it also explores their strengths, so Answer D is incorrect. Answer A is the best choice.

2. **C:** This term should be easy enough to define based on knowledge of the prefix and root; if not, scanning the text will reveal the answer. Answer B may be a deceptive choice since co-sleeping is associated with attachment parenting, but Answer C is the strongest response.

3. **C:** The final sentence of the last paragraph reads, "In the end, parents must rely on the only tried and true technique: trial and error." Only Answer C is consistent with this statement. Answer A is not addressed in the passage, and Answers B and C are at odds with the final sentence.

4. **A:** Answer A is the only answer with any connection to Ferber's "cry it out" method. Answer B is closer to the "attachment parenting" method. Answers C and D are not mentioned in the text.

5. **C:** While the term "contradictory" implies something that might be false (Answer A), deceitful (Answer B), or even inexact (Answer D), the meaning in the sentence is closest to Answer C, conflicting.

6. **B:** Answer A is incorrect because it is closer to Dr. Ferber's "cry it out" method. Answers C and D are not mentioned in the text. Answer B is the best answer.

7. **B:** In the sentence, the word "callous" is paired with the word "uncaring," the closest synonym of which is Answer B. Answers A and C are antonyms of "callous." Answer D is loosely connected to the discussion, but it is not a close synonym of "callous."

8. **D:** Answer D is implied in the last sentence, which suggests that parents use trial and error to figure out what works for them. Answers A and B are not directly addressed in the passage; Answer C may be implied, but it is not the main idea.

9. **B:** This question asks about the purpose of the passage. Just scanning the first word of each answer can help determine the best choice. This passage attempts to explain, not persuade or argue. Whereas answer D sounds somewhat true, the passage does not so much teach the process as give a brief overview. Answer B is the best choice.

10. **A:** Answer A is closest to the meaning of the word as used in the sentence. Whereas Answers B and D may both be related to the term, they are not adequate substitutes for it. Answer C is related to the discussion in paragraph 3, but not to this particular word.

11. **D:** Answer D is the only statement whose truth can be established by reading the passage. Answer A is not addressed in the passage. Answers B and C contain extreme, all-inclusive words like "all" and "only," which are red flags for an untrue statement.

12. **C:** Only Answer C is justified by the last paragraph. Answer A seems related to the paragraph, but it exaggerates. Answer B and D are not stated anywhere in the paragraph or the passage.

13. C: The meaning of the term "reverb" can be found in the sentence that reads, "The mixer will choose […] whether to add certain textures to the sound, such as <u>reverb</u> or echo, which both make some instruments sound further away than others." Answers A and B are somewhat deceptive because they sound like they might be related to the term. The word starts with the prefix "re-," which generally means to repeat something, so answer A is appealing. Answer B starts with the same prefix and is also tempting. Both are incorrect, though, as a quick scan of the sentence in the passage will reveal. Answer D is inconsistent with the passage.

14. A: Answer A is the only statement that can be logically deduced from the paragraph. Answers B, C, and D are not stated in the passage. Answer D may seem momentarily tempting because it sounds like it can be logically inferred from the paragraph, but a closer reading will discredit this answer; so will the fact that it is far from true.

15. A: Again, the answer can be found by scanning the sentence that contains the word. The sentence reads, "<u>Samples,</u> short recorded sounds triggered by a computer or keyboard."

16. D: This question will likely require you to read each answer carefully. It asks you to remember specific information from each of the paragraphs. Answer D is confirmed by the first sentence in paragraph 2, "Recording involves using microphones." None of the other statements can be confirmed by reading the passage.

17. B: In the sentence, "If you've ever seen the white <u>condensation</u> that rises above a pot of boiling water, then you've seen a cloud up close," the word "steam" could easily replace the word condensation. Answers A and D are incompatible with the sentence. Answer C, though related in meaning, is not as appropriate as Answer B, steam.

18. A: Answer A is the only sentence that is fully supported by the passage. Answers B, C, and D are not discussed in the passage.

19. C: This answer can be deduced from the sentence containing the word "currents." The sentence reads, "The <u>currents</u> of air in the atmosphere hold these tiny droplets up." Answers A and B, though they are both associated with the word "currents," are not mentioned anywhere in the passage. Answer D, "Vapor," though relevant to the discussion, is not mentioned as something that can hold up tiny droplets of water.

20. C: Answer C is the only answer that captures the main idea of the passage as a whole. The other answers reflect various ideas implied within specific paragraphs but not the overall passage.

21. A: This question addresses how the passage is written. Answer A is correct because the three questions provide a brief preview of the rest of the passage, in effect giving an overview of the passage's organization. Answer B is incorrect and answers C and D are easy to eliminate because they use words like "all" and "always."

22. D: Answer D is the only statement that can be correctly inferred from the paragraph. Answer A contradicts the paragraph; B and C are not mentioned in the paragraph.

23. B: Answer B is the only answer that is consistent with the information presented in the passage. The fourth paragraph reads, "When sunlight [...] passes through the tiny droplets in a cloud, it scatters all the different colors of light in every direction." Answers A, C, and D are not addressed in the passage.

24. B: Paragraph 2 states, "This vapor is invisible until it reaches higher levels of the atmosphere, where the temperature is much colder. There the water vapor begins to cool down and turn back into tiny droplets of water." Answer B is the only answer that fits with this explanation. Answer A may sound true, but it is not mentioned in the passage. Answers C and D are inconsistent with the passage, not to mention untrue.

25. A: Answer A is the best answer because the question asks for the main topic. Each of the other answers addresses the specific examples used in the paragraph, not the main topic.

26. B: The sentence in which the word is found reads, "There [in Persia] he allied himself with a local governor, or satrap." A quick scan of this sentence and the one preceding it should help eliminate all the other answers.

27. C: While any of these answers could account for Alcibiades' murder, only Answer C is accurate. Since the final paragraph mentions two accounts of Alcibiades' death, the best inference is that we don't know which one is true.

28. A: Only answer A is consistent with the meaning of the sentence the word is found in. Answers B and C are both related to the passage, but not the word. Answer D is far-fetched.

29. C: The use of the phrase "by coincidence" in the first sentence of the third paragraph helps us rule out answers A and D. No mention is made of the satrap in relation to Alcibiades' castle, so we can rule out Answer B. The process of elimination, as well as a quick scan of the end of paragraph three and the beginning of paragraph four, leaves us with choice C.

30. A: Like many other questions about the purpose of a passage, a quick glance at the first word of each answer can help eliminate incorrect answers. The passage is not written to persuade, which rules out Answer B; nor does it put forth much argumentation or reasoning, which rules out Answers C and D.

31. D: An ally is a confidant, so Answer D is the best choice. Answer A can be eliminated because the passage makes no mention of spying on the satrap. Answers C and D are tempting because they are related to the passage, but neither answer is in keeping with the meaning of the word "ally."

32. B: Answer B is the only answer that is broad enough to apply to the passage as a whole. Answers A and D are too narrow. Answer C may be broad enough, but nowhere in the passage does it mention Alcibiades' desire to become king.

33. C: Whereas in paragraph three this passage does touch on the debatable interpretations of quantum weirdness, the passage is not overtly trying to prove a point. Instead it is attempting to inform the reader of the unusual properties of the subatomic realm. Answer C is the best choice.

34. A: Answer A is the correct answer, though Answers B and D may be tempting because of the shared roots among "physics," "physiology," and "physical education." Answer C is a red herring; while it is true that some physicists study subatomic particles, the best choice is still Answer A.

35. A: In the passage, the number is followed by the statement, "This is a very small number," which is the equivalent of "a minuscule number," Answer A. Answers C and D are not mentioned anywhere in the passage.

36. B: Answers A and C are easy to eliminate because of the extreme wording. Answer D is unfounded based on the passage. Answer B is the best answer based on paragraph 3.

37. C: Answer C is easy to derive from the prefix and root of the word subatomic. Answers A and D can be eliminated because no mention of molecules is made in the passage. Answer B is related to the discussion in paragraph 3, but is incorrect.

38. C: Scanning the sentence containing the word should reveal the answer. Answers A and D are far-fetched; Answer B is deceptive, but again there is no mention of molecules in the passage.

39. A: Scanning the first word of each answer does not help with the process of elimination because each one starts with "some." Answer A best captures the sentence's meaning. Answers B and C are inconsistent with the meaning of the paragraph; Answer D sounds far-fetched and should be easy to eliminate.

40. C: Answer A is unlikely because of its all-inclusive wording. Answer B contradicts the final sentence of the passage. Answer D is inconsistent with the passage as a whole. Answer C is the most plausible answer.

Reading Vocabulary

41. C: Skulk means to move about in a stealthy manner or sneak.

42. B: Smoldering means to burn without flames or smoke heavily.

43. A: Mulish is the adjectival form of the noun "mule," and means stubborn.

44. D: A hypocritical person is someone whose actions contradict the values they hold others to. Insincere is the closest synonym in this list.

45. B: Jubilation means great happiness, or elation.

46. B: Belated means overdue or untimely.

47. A: Monopolize means to dominate or to corner a market.

48. A: Faltering means hesitating or wavering.

49. B: Unanimous means undisputed.

50. C: <u>Imminent</u> means <u>about to happen</u> or <u>soon-to-occur</u>. It is often confused with its homonym, eminent, which means highly esteemed and admired.

51. B: <u>Radiate</u> means to spread out in every direction. The closest synonym here is <u>shine.</u>

52. D: <u>Bountiful</u> means overabundant or <u>plentiful.</u>

53. A: The nearest synonym to <u>listless</u> in this list is <u>lethargic</u>.

54. B: <u>Heritage</u> can refer literally to an inheritance, or more broadly to a culture's <u>traditions</u>.

55. D: The closest synonym to <u>compel</u> is <u>influence</u>.

56. A: <u>Persistent</u> most nearly means <u>ongoing</u>.

57. B: <u>Defaced</u> means <u>vandalized</u>.

58. D: Whereas several of these choices could be associated with <u>tariffs</u> or the people who create them, the closest synonym is <u>tax</u>.

59. A: <u>Disadvantaged</u> most nearly means <u>deprived</u>.

60. A: <u>Proclamation</u> most nearly means edict or <u>announcement</u>.

61. B: <u>Artificial</u> most nearly means <u>synthetic</u>.

62. C: : The closest synonym to <u>particle</u> is <u>element</u>.

Language

Usage, Punctuation and Grammar

1. B: Comma. The comma in front of the phrase "the German shepherd" sets it off, and it must be followed by a comma as well.

2. D: None of the sentences contains an error.

3. A: Fragment. Though this sentence contains a subject, "population," it contains no predicate.

4. C: Pronoun-antecedent agreement.   The pronoun "his" does not agree with its antecedent, "farmers."

5. B: Comma splice. There are really two sentences here, one before and one after the comma. Two complete sentences joined together with a comma is a comma splice. Sentence A contains an apostrophe that might throw some readers for a moment, but closer reading will show that the word neighbors can be plural in this sentence, so the apostrophe is in the correct position.

6. D: None of the sentences contains an error.

7. C: Subject-verb disagreement. Despite the word "there" at the beginning, "vegetables" is the real subject of this sentence. When the words "there is" or "there are" come at the beginning of a sentence, the verb ("is" or "are") should always agree with the subject of the sentence. In this case, the subject is "vegetables," and the verb should be "are" because "vegetables" is plural.

8. C: Subject-verb disagreement. The verb of this sentence is "remembers," and the subject is "Students." When there is a long clause in between the subject and the verb of a sentence, it's easy to miss the subject-verb disagreement.

9. C: Adverb/Adjective. The adverb "separately" should be written as the adjective "separate."

10. B: Fused sentence. Sentence B is known as a fused sentence or a run-on. It contains two sentences jammed together with no punctuation.

11. D: None of these sentences contains a mistake.

12. D: None of these sentences contains a mistake.

13. C: Subject-verb disagreement. The pronoun "no one" is always singular. Here the verb "were" is plural and does not agree with "no one."

14. A: Verb tense. The verb in the first clause of the sentence is in the past tense, but the verb at the end is in present. "Get" should read "got."

15. A: Subject-verb disagreement. "Kills" is a singular verb, but it does not agree with the plural "fishermen," which is the subject of the sentence.

16. A: Comma splice. Sentence A is a comma splice because it fuses two complete sentences together with a comma.

17. B: Apostrophe. The apostrophe on the word "Congress'" does not need to be there.

18. B: Double negative. The phrase "couldn't hardly" is nonstandard because it forms a double negative.

19. C: Fragment. Sentence 19 is a dependent clause, which cannot stand on its own.

20. B: Subject-verb disagreement. The subject of the sentence is a compound plural, "night and day," and it requires a plural verb. The sentence should read, "night and day are the same length."

21. C: Comma splice. These two sentences are fused together with a comma, making this sentence a comma splice.

22. B: Subject-verb disagreement. The plural verb "mow" does not agree with the singular subject, "Pete."

23. C: Punctuation. Though the sentence talks about a question, the sentence is itself declarative and requires a period.

24. A: Capitalization. The word "People" does not need to be capitalized.

25. C: Comma. There should be a comma to separate the digits in the date at the end of this sentence.

26. A: Capitalization. "African" should be capitalized.

27. A: Subject-verb disagreement. The compound subject is "Belgium, The Netherlands, and Luxembourg" and requires a plural verb. The singular verb "is" does not agree with the plural subject.

28. D: None of these sentences contains a mistake.

29. C: Fused sentence. This sentence is a run-on or a fused sentence. It joins two complete sentences without any punctuation.

30. C: Verb. Since "to write" is in the infinitive form, the verb should not take an ending. "To writes" is incorrect.

31. D: None of the sentences is incorrect.

32. A: Capitalization. The word "house" does not need to be capitalized.

33. B: Apostrophe. The contraction "couldn't" requires an apostrophe between the "n" and the "t."

34. A: Verb. "Hitted" is incorrect verb usage.

35. D: None of these sentences contains a mistake.

36. C: Comma. The list of words at the end of this sentence needs commas to separate each item.

37. D:None of these sentences contains a mistake.

38. B: Comma. There is no need to place a comma in the middle of this sentence.

39. A: Capitalization. The word "soprano" does not need to be capitalized.

40. B: Comma. The list in the middle of this sentence requires commas after the words "toothpaste" and "toothbrush."

41. D: None of these sentences contains a mistake.

42. C: Verb. "Mights" is not a correct verb form.

Spelling

43. B: The word "then" is incorrect in this context. It should be "than."

44. A: The word "garrage" should be spelled "garage."

45. D: None of the sentences contains a spelling mistake.

46. B: "Soul" should be spelled "sole."

47. D: None of these sentences contains a spelling mistake.

48. A: "Loosing" should be spelled "losing."

49. C: "Neice" should be spelled "niece."

50. B: "Evenning" only has one "n" and should read "evening."

Composition

51. B: The sentence fits best after sentence 2 because it explicitly refers back to the terms used in sentence 2. The phrase "problematic beliefs" shows up in both sentences.

52. D: The sentence fits best after sentence 4 because it contains a statement that directly contrasts with the statement made in sentence 4.

53. A: Since the second part of the clause contrasts with the first part, the conjunction "but" is the best choice.

54. B: All of the choices except for "because" indicate contrast, but these two clauses do not contrast with each other.

55. A: Since the two clauses contrast with each other, "but" is the best choice.

56. C: All of the sentences except for sentence C are confusingly worded and written in the passive voice.

57. B: All of the sentences except B are poorly worded or they contain verb errors.

58. A: All of the sentences except A are poorly worded or they contain verb errors.

59. C: Sentence 4 is only tangentially related to the discussion of recycling rubber tires.

60. A: The sentence about Bob Dylan's best records is not directly relevant to the discussion, nor is it consistent with the tone of the discussion.

Quantitative Skills

1. B: $\dfrac{90}{3} = 30$, and 30 + 6 = 36.

2. A: Each element of the series is a multiple of 3 less than the previous element. Starting with 116, the next element is 1 × 3 less, or 116 – (1 × 3) = 113. The next element is 2 × 3 less, or 113 – (2 × 3) = 107. The next element is 3 × 3 less, or 107 – (3 × 3) = 98. So the next element will be 4 × 3 less, or 98 – (4 × 3) = 86.

3. A: Since $\dfrac{1}{5}$ of 30 = 6, $\dfrac{1}{4}$ of 20 = 5, and $\dfrac{1}{3}$ of 15 = 5, it follows that (a) > (b) = (c).

4. B: Since 12 × 3 = 36, there are 36 inches in a yard. Solving 2.5 × 36 = 90 shows that B is correct.

5. D: $\dfrac{117}{13} = 9$. Dividing any of the other choices by 11 will leave a remainder.

6. C: Since $2^3 = 2 \times 2 \times 2 = 8$, and 3 × 8 = 24, C is correct.

7. C: Since A is at the intersection of the diagonals, the regions II and III are both quadrants of the square and are equal. Region I is one half of the square and is equal to two quadrants, so it is greater than II or III.

8. D: Following the normal order of operations, first calculate the sum in the grouping symbols: 2 + 3 = 5. The expression is then equivalent to 9 + 4 × 5. Next multiply or divide, which makes the expression 9 + 20. Finally add to find that 9 + 20 = 29.

9. C: 24% is equivalent to $\dfrac{24}{100}$, which is equal to $\dfrac{12}{50}$. The decimal 0.24 is equivalent to $\dfrac{0.24}{1} = \dfrac{24}{100}$, which is the same as the preceding examples. However, $\dfrac{24}{10}$ is 10 times greater than $\dfrac{24}{100}$, so it is not equivalent to the other expressions.

10. A: First, evaluate the expressions within the grouping symbols, starting from the innermost and working outwards. This yields 3 + [(3)•6] – 20 = 3 + 18 – 20 = 1.

11. C: Since 3 × 9 = 27, and 45 – 27 = 18, then 45 – 18 = 27 and choice C is correct.

12. B: In this series, 5 and 4 are added alternatively to successive numbers to determine the next numeral: 54 + 5 = 59, 59 + 4 = 63, etc. Since 68 + 4 = 72, the next element is calculated by adding 5: 72 + 5 = 77, so that choice B is correct.

13. C: Since 1/3 = 0.33, and 2/3 = 0.66, the correct answer must lie between 0.33 and 0.66. Only choice C satisfies this condition.

14. D: Since there are 12 inches in a foot, then 4 inches is equal to $\dfrac{4}{12} = \dfrac{1}{3}$ foot.

- 67 -

15. B: The series consists of a series of numbers each of which is double the preceding number. Since 2 × 8 = 16, choice B is correct.

16. C: In an isosceles triangle, two of the sides are congruent, and two of the angles are congruent. In this case, since side AB is congruent to side AC (and side BC is shorter), thus the angles B and C are congruent and greater than the measure of angle A.

17. D: Since 23 × 4 = 92 exactly, 92 is a multiple of 23. All other answers do not have 23 as a factor.

18. A: A prime number is divisible only by itself and by one. Of the even numbers, only 2 is prime. The number 76 is divisible by 2, 4, 19, and 38 in addition to 1 and itself.

19. B: Since $\dfrac{66}{3} = 22$, and 11 + 11 = 22, then 11 added to itself is 1/3 of 66.

20. C: The series represents increasing powers of 3: 3^1, 3^2, 3^3, etc. Since $81 = 3^4$, the next element in the series will be 3^5, which is 243. Expressed differently, each number in the series is triple the preceding number, and 81 × 3 = 243.

21. C: The subtraction of a negative number is equivalent to the addition of its positive conjugate, so that -4 – (-10) is the same as -4 + 10 = 6. For the other choices, 6 – 2 = 4; -4 – 2 = -6; and 11 – 6 = 5. Of 6, 4, -6, and 5, 6 is the greatest.

22. A: To average a group of numbers, take the sum and divide by the number of items. The average of the numbers given is $\dfrac{7+14+22+23}{4} = 16.5$. One half of this number is 8.25.

23. B: The area of a rectangle is given by A = width × length. The area of a triangle is given by A = $\dfrac{height \times base}{2}$. In the figure, the height of the triangle equals the length of the rectangle, and the base of the triangle, BC, equals the width of the rectangle, AB. Therefore the triangle's height × base equals the rectangle's width × length and, since the area of a triangle is half that amount, that area is also half the area of the rectangle.

24. B: The product of any number and an even number must be even. Therefore, the first product will be even. The second multiplication produces the product of this even number and an odd number, which must also be even.

25. C: A number less than zero is a negative number, and the product of two negative numbers must be positive.

26. C: In this series, the interval between successive numbers increases by an amount that is one less than the previous interval. Thus, 23 – 18 = 5, 27 – 23 = 4, 30 – 27 = 3. Therefore, the next number should be 27 + 2, or 29.

27. D: The expression within the grouping symbols must be evaluated first: 6 + 1 = 7. This result is then multiplied by the number outside the grouping symbols: 4 × 7 = 28. Since $\frac{56}{2} = 28$, answer choice D is correct.

28. C: A prime number can be factored only by itself and by 1. Since the product of two prime numbers can be factored by either of the primes, it cannot be prime itself.

29. D: If both numbers are positive, and the greater one is subtracted from the smaller, the result must be less than zero, or negative.

30. B: The expressions within the grouping symbols must be evaluated first, yielding (4)(3). Since 4 × 3 = 12, answer choice B is correct.

31. C: A quadrilateral with two pair of equal, opposite sides is called a parallelogram. In all such figures, which include squares and rectangles, the measures of the opposite angles are equal to one another.

32. A: Since 36 – 17 = 19, and 3 × 19 = 57, choice A is correct.

33. C: Since 8 × 8 = 64, and 64 – 5 is 59, choice C is correct.

34. B: Since $4^3 = 4 \times 4 \times 4 = 64$, and $5^2 = 5 \times 5 = 25$, and $3^4 = 3 \times 3 \times 3 \times 3 = 81$, and since 64 > 27 < 81, it follows that choice B is correct.

35. B: In this series, each term is double the previous term. For example, 14 = 2 × 7, and 28 = 2 × 14. The next term must be 2 × 56 = 112, so that choice B is correct.

36. D: Since $\frac{2}{3} \times 66 = 44$, and $\frac{88}{2} = 44$, answer D is correct.

37. D: "Percent" means "parts per 100", so that 30% of 90 is $\frac{30}{100} \times 90 = 27$. Similarly, 10% of 270 is $\frac{10}{100} \times 270 = 27$, and 60% of 45 is $\frac{60}{100} \times 45 = 27$ so that all three expressions are equal.

38. C: Since 4 × 5 = 20, and 6 × 20 = 120, then $\frac{120}{2} = 60$ and answer choice C is right.

39. C: To compare the fractions, express them with a common denominator. This is done by multiplying each fraction's numerator and denominator by the denominator of the other. Therefore, $\frac{2}{3} \times \frac{4}{4} = \frac{8}{12}$, and $\frac{3}{4} \times \frac{3}{3} = \frac{9}{12}$. The correct answer must lie between these two numbers. Since $\frac{8}{12} = \frac{16}{24}$, and $\frac{9}{12} = \frac{18}{24}$, choice C, which is between these two numbers, is correct.

40. D: To find a number that is halfway between two others, add the numbers and divide by 2. This gives $\frac{\frac{2}{9} + \frac{5}{9}}{2} = \frac{\frac{7}{9}}{2} = \frac{7}{18}$.

41. A: In this series, each term is equal to 3 added to the previous term, for example -3 = 3 + -6, and 0 = 3 + -3. Therefore, the following term must be equal to 3 + 0, which is 3.

42. C: When two line segments intersect, vertical angles are congruent and adjacent angles are supplementary, thus the sum of their measures if 180°. Therefore, $A = C$ and $B = D$, which is choice C.

43. A: A number immediately next to a bracketing symbol multiplies the expression within the brackets. All three expressions are equal to 224.

44. C: Since 7 × 6 = 42, and 42 – 8 = 34, choice C is correct.

45. D: "Percent" means "parts per 100", so that 125% of 20 is equal to $\frac{125}{100} \times 20 = 25$.

46. B: "Percent" means "parts per 100", so that 15% of 70 is equal to $\frac{15}{100} \times 70 = 10.5$. Two times 10.5 is equal to 21, so that choice B is correct.

47. B: In this series, each term is equal to 12 less than the previous term. For example, 1999 – 12 = 1987 and 1987 – 12 = 1975. Therefore, the following term must be equal to 1975 – 12, which is equal to 1963.

48. B: The only integer between 4 and 6 is 5, so (a) must equal 5. Half of 10 is 5, so (b) must equal 5. The only prime number between 3 and 7 is 5, so (c) must equal 5. Since all 3 items equal 5, choice B is correct.

49. C: The average of 10, 12, and 14 is $\frac{10 + 12 + 14}{3} = 12$. Since 3 × 4 = 12, and one-half of 8 = 4, choice C is correct.

50. D: Since "percent" means "parts per 100", 90% is equal to $\dfrac{90}{100} = \dfrac{9}{10}$. The decimal expression 0.9 is also equal to $\dfrac{9}{10}$, so (a) and (c) are equal. However, $\dfrac{1}{9} \neq \dfrac{9}{10}$, so choice D is correct.

51. D: Even numbers must be integers, so the result cannot be a fraction. Only one even number, 2, is prime, so the result cannot be prime. The product of any number and an even number must be even, so the result cannot be odd, and choice D must be correct.

52. A: Since 0.8 × 0.7 = 0.56, and 0.08 × 0.07 = 0.0056, and 0.008 × 0.007 = 0.000056, choice A is correct.

Mathematics

1. C: The decimal expression 0.20 is equal to $\frac{20}{100}$, which is equivalent to $\frac{1}{5}$, as can be seen by dividing both numerator and denominator by 20.

2. B: Since 18 = 6 × 3, choice B is correct. All of the other choices leave a remainder when divided by 6.

3. D: Fractions having a denominator equal to zero are not defined in the set of real numbers.

4. A: Choices B and D are not prime numbers, so they cannot be prime factors of 121. 121 is not divisible by 13, so choice C is also incorrect. However 11 × 11 = 121, and 11 is prime, so that choice A is correct.

5. B: Rounding to the nearest tenth means adjusting the first digit after the decimal to the value closest to the actual calculated answer, and then truncating the answer at that digit. Since 4.171 + 4.55 = 8.721, 8.7 is closer than 8.8, so that choice B is correct.

6. B: Each term in the sequence is equal to 3 raised to a power equal to its position in the sequence. For example, the third term is equal to $3^3 = 27$.

7. B: Any number raised to the power of 0 is equal to 1.

8. A: The correct answer s A. Since $\frac{1}{3} = \frac{10}{30} = \frac{100}{300}$ and, for example, $\frac{10}{30} > \frac{10}{33}$ (the first fraction having the larger denominator), choice A is the greatest.

9. C: Since $\frac{\$30}{2} = \$15$, choice C is correct.

10. D: If the perimeter P = 44 cm, then the side of the square $a = \frac{P}{4} = \frac{44}{4} = 11$. Since the area of a square $A = a^2$, then $A = 11^2 = 11 \times 11 = 121$.

11. B: Since 3 + 9 = 12, Sandra has $9.

12. B: "Bisect" means to divide exactly in half. Therefore, the measure of ∠BAD is twice as large as the measure of ∠BAC. Since 2 × 15 = 30, choice B is correct.

13. D: The average temperature in October is 26°C, and in November it is 16°C, a difference of 10°C. This is the steepest decline on the graph.

14. A: The correct answer is A. Multiplying an expression enclosed in grouping symbols by -1 changes the sign of all of the terms within the grouping symbols. Therefore $-1(x - y) = (-x + y) = (y - x)$.

15. B: The "5" in 452 occupies the tens place and represents the number of tens in the number, or 5 × 10.

16. D: The coordinates of points in a Cartesian plane are represented in the form (x,y). The point A in the figure is at $x = 2$ and $y = 3$ and is represented as (2,3).

17. B: To add the expressions, add each pair of like terms. This yields $2y - y = y$; $3x + 3x = 6x$; and $11 + 4 = 15$. Combine these sums to form choice B.

18. C: The expression is equivalent to $4 + 7 + \dfrac{2}{3} + \dfrac{1}{5} = 11 + \dfrac{2}{3} + \dfrac{1}{5}$. To add the mixed fractions, first convert them to the least common denominator by multiplying each fraction by the denominator of the other: $\dfrac{2}{3} + \dfrac{1}{5} = \dfrac{2(5)}{3(5)} + \dfrac{1(3)}{5(3)} = \dfrac{13}{15}$. Now combine the terms: $11\dfrac{13}{15}$.

19. B: Calculate the perimeter for each shape. For the square, $P = 4 \times 3 = 12$. For the circle, $P = 2\pi \times 3 = 18.85$. For the rectangle, $P = 2 \times (1 + 4) = 10$. For the triangle, $P = 3 \times 3 = 9$.

20. D: The total weight in ounces is $12 \times 6 = 72$ ounces. Divide 72 by the number of ounces per pound: $\dfrac{72}{16} = 4$ with a remainder of 8 ounces.

21. A: For every 3 cats, there are 2 dogs. Therefore, divide the number of cats by 3 and multiply by 2 to get the answer: $45 \times \dfrac{2}{3} = 30$.

22. B: In scientific notation, a negative exponent means that the decimal must be moved to the left by the number of digits indicated by the value of the exponent. Moving the decimal 3 digits to the left starting with 5.12 yields 0.00512.

23. C: The difference between -2.95 and -3 is 0.05. All the other differences are greater.

24. C: The product of two odd numbers must be odd. The product of a positive number and a negative number must be negative.

25. D: The ratio 2:5 is equivalent to the ratio 40:100, which is equivalent to 40%. In fractional notation, $\dfrac{2}{5} = \dfrac{40}{100}$, and since "percent" means "parts per 100", answer D is correct.

26. C: The area of a rectangle is the product of its length by its width. Since the length and width are given, multiply $3.4 \times 5.7 = 19.38$.

27. D: Tom's total at the end of the year will consist of the interest earned added to the original amount, or principal, that he deposited. The interest is 7% of $3800, $\dfrac{7 \times 3800}{100}$, or $266. Adding this amount to the original amount deposited, $3800, yields a total of $4066.

28. D: To calculate this, first determine the number of man-hours required to paint the room. This is the number of hours it would take a single man to do the job. Since two men do the job in 8 hours, it takes $2 \times 8 = 16$ man-hours to paint the room. If 5 men work on the job, the total time

required will be 16/5 = 3.2 hours. Since 0.2 hour, or 1/5th of an hour, equals 12 minutes $(\frac{60}{5}=12)$, answer D is correct

29. B: Each of the answer choices expresses a number as the product of N and a factor. The values of the factors 0.2, 20%, and 1/5 are all the same, since $20\%=\frac{20}{100}=\frac{1}{5}$, and $0.2=\frac{2}{10}=\frac{1}{5}$. Only 20 is different from the others, so that choice B is correct.

30. D: Since "%" means "parts per 100", cell phone users are $\frac{240}{100}$ times as likely to have tumors as other people, for whom the rate is 12 per 100,000. The answer is therefore $12\times\frac{240}{100}=28.8$ per 100,000.

31. A: This equation is in the standard format for a linear equation. The number of hours, H, is multiplied by a factor that indicates the slope of the line, or rate of change, which is 4°F per hour. It shows the temperature starting at 70° F, which is the y-intercept, or the temperature when $h = 0$.

32. C: The shaded area represents the difference between the area of the square and that of the circle. Since the circle is inscribed within the square, the side of the square is equal to $2R$, where R equals the radius, so that its area is $4R^2$. The area of the circle is πR^2. The shaded area is the difference between these two quantities, or $4R^2-\pi R^2=R^2(4-\pi)$.

33. C: Replace the variables with their assigned values and compute the value of the expression following the normal order of operations. With the values substituted for the variables the expression becomes $3(3)^2+2(7)=27+14=41$.

34. A: The quotient of two radicals can be computed by placing the entire quotient under the radical sign and then simplifying. In this case, $\frac{\sqrt{40}}{\sqrt{2}}=\sqrt{\frac{40}{2}}=\sqrt{20}$ .Note that $\sqrt{20}=\sqrt{4\bullet5}=2\sqrt{5}$, so choice C and D are both incorrect.

35. B: The problem may be solved arithmetically or algebraically. To solve it arithmetically, divide 123 by 3, which yields 41. This is the middle integer. The other two must be (41 - 1) = 40, and (41+ 1) = 42. To solve the problem algebraically, let the first integer be x. Then, since the integers are consecutive, $x+(x+1)+(x+2)=123$, or $3x+3=123$. Subtracting 3 from both sides of this equation yields $3x=120$, so that $x = 40$.

36. C: The result for each toss is independent of the results for any other toss. For a single coin, the probability of tossing heads is 1/2. For all three coins to come up heads, the probability is the product of the probabilities for each individual trial, or $P=\frac{1}{2}\times\frac{1}{2}\times\frac{1}{2}=\frac{1}{8}$.

37. B: Since the two lines are parallel, it follows that the angles δ and θ are equal to one another. The angles α and θ are supplementary angles. That is, they add up to 180°. It follows that θ = 180 - α = 180 - 135 = 45°, and since δ = θ, then δ = 45°.

38. B: The perimeter of a circle is given by $P = 2\pi R$, where R is the radius. If the CD rotates at 500 RPM, the point on the periphery moves the length of 500 perimeters every minute, or 500P. A point halfway between the center and the perimeter is at a radial position $r = \dfrac{R}{2}$. As it rotates, it describes a circle of perimeter $p = 2\pi r = 2\pi \dfrac{R}{2} = \dfrac{P}{2}$, and it moves the length of 500p every minute. Since $500p = \dfrac{500P}{2}$, this is half the distance moved by the first point, and the speed of the inner point is 1/2 the speed of the outer point, or $\dfrac{470}{2} = 235$.

39. D: Multiply the average speed by the elapsed time to find the answer: 2.5 × 36 = 90 miles.

40. B: Since $\dfrac{3}{5}$ of the vehicles are trucks, the remaining vehicles comprise $1 - \dfrac{3}{5} = \dfrac{2}{5}$ of the fleet. Since the entire fleet is 60 vehicles, $\dfrac{2}{5} \times 60 = 24$ vehicles are compact cars. One half of these will be replaced by hybrids, or $\dfrac{24}{2} = 12$.

41. B: Kevin has 12 shirts in all. The chance of selecting a blue shirt is $\dfrac{2}{12}$, since 2 of the shirts are blue. Likewise, the chance of selecting a red shirt is $\dfrac{4}{12}$, since 4 of the shirts are red. The probability of selecting either red or blue is the sum of these two probabilities: $\dfrac{2}{12} + \dfrac{4}{12} = \dfrac{6}{12} = \dfrac{1}{2}$, which is equal to 50%.

42. C: Divide the total in Andrea's account at the end of the year by the total number of deposits: $\dfrac{1560}{52} = 30$. This is the amount she saved each week. Since this amount represents 10% of her paycheck, and since $10\% = \dfrac{10}{100}$, divide the amount by 10% to calculate her total pay: $\dfrac{30}{\frac{10}{100}} = 30 \times \dfrac{100}{10} = \$300$.

43. D: To compute the average, or arithmetic mean, of a group of numbers, add them together and then divide by the total number of items. Since there are 4 scores in the table, this yields $\dfrac{83 + 88 + 92 + 93}{4} = \dfrac{356}{4} = 89$.

44. D: The formula for the area of a triangle, A, is $A = \dfrac{1}{2}hB$, where h is the height and B is the base. Here, the base is equal to 4. For a right triangle, as in this case, the height is equal to the length of one of the sides. The length of the vertical side in the figure is also equal to 4. Substituting these numbers into the formula yields $A = \dfrac{1}{2}(4 \times 4) = \dfrac{1}{2}(16) = 8$.

45. C: To compute the average, or arithmetic mean, of a group of numbers, add them together and then divide by the total number of items. In this case, set up the equations for the two averages and set them to be equal: $\dfrac{6+8+x}{3} = \dfrac{x+12}{2}$. To solve this equation, first eliminate the denominators. Multiply each fraction by the other fraction's denominator: $2(6+8+x) = 3(x+12)$. Use the distributive property to get: $12+16+2x = 3x+36$. Gather like terms to get: $-8 = x$.

46. B: Solve this equation by isolating the variable on one side of the equality sign. Start by dividing both sides of the equation by 3, which yields $4x + 3 = 15$. Next, subtract 3 from both sides, which yields $4x = 12$. Finally, divide both sides by 4, leaving the variable, x, isolated on one side and yielding $x = 3$.

47. C: Following normal order of operations, start by calculating the expression inside the brackets. Calculate the power first: $3^2 = 9$, so that the bracketed expression equals 44 + 9 = 53. Next, evaluate $2^2 = 4$. Finally, add the expressions, which yields 53 + 4 = 57.

48. B: If B and C are the centers of the two circles, then both line segments AB and CD are equal to the radius r. The segment BC is also equal to r, and represents the overlap of the radii of both circles. So, the total length of AD is the sum of these lengths, or $r + r + r = 3r$.

49. A: The average of a set of terms is their sum divided by the number of terms. Reversing this, the sum is the product of the average and the number of terms, so that Charlotte's scores for the first three tests totaled 3 × 86 = 258. After four tests, her scores must have totaled 4 × 88 = 352 if her average rose to 88. Therefore, her score on the fourth test was 352 – 258 = 94.

50. C: $25 is equivalent to 100% - 80% = 20% of the original price P. Since "percent" means "parts per 100", then $\dfrac{25}{P} = \dfrac{20}{100}$. To solve this proportion, multiply both sides by P and by 100, which yields 25 × 100 = 20P. Now, divide both sides of this equation by 20, which yields the final answer, $P = \$125$.

51. A: Factor the expression to yield $\sqrt{40} = \sqrt{4(10)} = \sqrt{4(2)(5)}$. Remove the perfect square from the radicand, the expression under the radical sign, by taking its square root: $\sqrt{4(2)(5)} = 2\sqrt{2(5)} = 2\sqrt{2}\sqrt{5}$.

52. A: The correct answer is A. Prime factors are prime numbers which can be multiplied to give the number in question. A prime number is one which can be factored only by itself and by 1. To factor 93, divide by the first available prime that is greater than 1. Since the number is not divisible by 2, divide by 3: 93 = 3 × 31. Since 31 is also a prime number, the process can be taken no further, and A is correct.

53. C: Since 4 × 17 = 68, and 72 − 68 = 4, then $\frac{72}{17} = 4 + \frac{4}{17}$. Since $\frac{4}{17} = \frac{1}{\frac{17}{4}}$, and 4 × 4 = 16, then

$\frac{17}{4} = 4 + \frac{1}{4}$. Substituting this expression into the one derived previously, $4 + \frac{4}{17} = 4 + \frac{1}{4 + \frac{1}{4}}$.

This type of expression is called a *continuing fraction*.

54. A: Isolate the variable q by multiplying both sides of the equation by the denominator, -16. This

yields $\frac{q}{-16}(-16) = -64(-16)$. Simplifying yields q = -64(-16). Since the product of two negative numbers is positive, q = 1024 and answer choice A is correct.

55. B: Following normal order of operations, evaluate the expressions in the inner-most grouping symbols first. Since 11 − 6 = 5, this yields 15 + (16 − [2(5)] -3). Since 2 × 5 = 10, this is equivalent to 15 + (16 − 10 − 3) = 15 + 3 = 18, and answer choice B is correct.

56. D: The shaded area is equal to the area of the square less one half the area of the circle. The square has a side of length 2r. Since the area of a square is equal to the length of the side

squared, this is 4r^2, or 4 × 16 = 64. The area of the circle is given by πr^2, and half the area is $\frac{\pi r^2}{2}$.

Since r^2 = 16, $\frac{\pi r^2}{2}$ = 8π. The shaded area is therefore 64 − 8π, = 8(8 − π).

57. C: To solve an equation where a variable is squared, it is possible to take the square root of both

sides. The square root of x^2 is x. The square root of $\frac{81}{4}$ is $\frac{\sqrt{81}}{\sqrt{4}} = \frac{9}{2}$.

58. D: The area of a square is the length of one side squared, so first calculate the side. The perimeter of a square is 4 times the length of the side, so the length of one side for this square is

$\frac{160}{4}$ = 40 m. to obtain the area, square this number with the result 40 × 40 − 1600 m².

59. D: First, determine the value of x. The decimal value 0.25 is equivalent to $\frac{1}{4}$, so that x is equal to

4. Since 17 − 4 = 13, y equals 13.

60. C: Since the product of two negative numbers is positive, the square root of a positive number can have two values. For example, 3 × 3 = 9, so that one value for $\sqrt{9}$ is +3. The second value is negative: -3 × -3 = 9, so that $\sqrt{9}$ may also be equal to -3.

61. C: Determine how much of the candle has been consumed by subtracting its present length from its original length: 21 − 9 = 12 cm. Since the candle is consumed at the rate of 3 cm per hour, divide the length that has been consumed by this rate to obtain the time it has been burning:

$\frac{12}{3}$ = 4 hours.

62. A: The total cost consists of the price, the tax, and the shipping. First, calculate the 10% tax, which is $\dfrac{10}{100} \times \$22 = \$2.20$. Add together all the elements of the cost: $22 + $2.20 + $4 = $28.20.

63. B: Since $4 \times 4 \times 4 \times 4 = 256$, then $256 = 4^4$ and we have $4^x = 4^4$. If the bases are equal in an equation, the exponents must be equal, as well. Therefore, $x = 4$.

64. B: The variable m is used to represent the amount of money that Monica has. One third of this is $\dfrac{m}{3}$. Since Pamela has $5 more than this, the amount she has can be expressed as $5 + \dfrac{m}{3}$.

Practice Test #2

Practice Questions

Verbal Skills

1. **Generous** most nearly means
    a. giving
    b. truthful
    c. selfish
    d. harsh

2. Elevator is to building as
    a. seat is to theater
    b. apple is to core
    c. fence is to fence post
    d. plumber is to pipes

3. Significant means the opposite of
    a. Trivial
    b. Important
    c. Major
    d. Considerable

4. Which word does not belong with the others?
    a. Chair
    b. Couch
    c. Bed
    d. Furniture

5. Lesley was born the year before Steve. Steve and Barb both have birthdays in September. Lesley is older than Barb. If the first two statements are true, then the third is:
    a. True
    b. False
    c. Unknown

6. Valuable means the opposite of
    a. Precious
    b. Costly
    c. Worthless
    d. Priceless

7. Which word does not belong with the others?
   a. Woman
   b. Man
   c. Girl
   d. Female

8. Coarse is to fine as
   a. soil is to earth
   b. buoyant is to airy
   c. fool is to foolish
   d. deliberate is to accidental

9. **Residence** most nearly means
   a. home
   b. area
   c. plan
   d. resist

10. Monica scored higher on the test than Ray. Ray outscored Juliet. Juliet scored higher on the test than Monica. If the first two statements are true, then the third is:
    a. True
    b. False
    c. Unknown

11. Annoying means the opposite of
    a. Maddening
    b. Pleasing
    c. Frustrating
    d. Irritating

12. Which word does not belong with the others?
    a. House
    b. Apartment
    c. Mobile Home
    d. Domicile

13. Flagrant means the opposite of
    a. Blatant
    b. Obvious
    c. Clear
    d. Obscure

14. **Gigantic** most nearly means
    a. small
    b. great
    c. huge
    d. scary

15. Ice is to skate as water is to
   a. lake
   b. wash
   c. drink
   d. swim

16. Righteous means the opposite of
   a. Evil
   b. Moral
   c. Honest
   d. Upstanding

17. Rocco is taller than Ashley. Brian is shorter than Ashley. Rocco is taller than Brian. If the first two statements are true, then the third is:
   a. True
   b. False
   c. Unknown

18. Flat means the opposite of
   a. Smooth
   b. Uneven
   c. Even
   d. Level

19. **Opportunity** most nearly means
   a. event
   b. plan
   c. direction
   d. chance

20. Global means the opposite of
   a. Worldwide
   b. Overall
   c. International
   d. Narrow

21. Driver is to truck as
   a. horse is to rider
   b. hiker is to trail
   c. waiter is to restaurant
   d. engineer is to train

22. Bill has more money than Stan. Randall has more money than Stan. Randall has more money than Bill. If the first two statements are true, then the third is:
   a. True
   b. False
   c. Unknown

23. Which word does not belong with the others?
   a. Poodle
   b. Boxer
   c. Cardinal
   d. Labrador

24. Morose means the opposite of
   a. Upbeat
   b. Depressed
   c. Down
   d. Sullen

25. Oblivious means the opposite of
   a. Unaware
   b. Uninformed
   c. Conscious
   d. Ignorant

26. **Frequently** most nearly means
   a. difficulty
   b. freely
   c. often
   d. easy

27. Reece weighs more than Scott. Scott is heavier than Della. Reece weighs more than Della. If the first two statements are true, then the third is:
   a. True
   b. False
   c. Unknown

28. Snow is to avalanche as
   a. hail is to rain
   b. lightening is to thunder
   c. water is to river
   d. wind is to tornado

29. Compact means the opposite of
   a. Dense
   b. Squashed
   c. Compressed
   d. Loose

30. Monday is my longest day at work. Tuesday is shorter than Thursday. Thursday is longer than Monday. If the first two statements are true, then the third is:
   a. True
   b. False
   c. Unknown

31. **Purchased** most nearly means
    a. sold
    b. bargained
    c. complained
    d. bought

32. Almost means the opposite of
    a. Nearly
    b. Exactly
    c. Practically
    d. Roughly

33. Cry is to sadness as
    a. fear is to function
    b. yell is to anger
    c. happiness is to smile
    d. doubt is to confusion

34. Change means the opposite of
    a. Remain
    b. Alter
    c. Amend
    d. Transform

35. **Entire** most nearly means
    a. whole
    b. divide
    c. tired
    d. basic

36. The football game lasted an hour longer than the baseball game. The soccer game was an hour longer than the football game. The baseball game took longer than the soccer game. If the first two statements are true, then the third is:
    a. True
    b. False
    c. Unknown

37. Water is to thirst as food is to
    a. crop
    b. feast
    c. hunger
    d. fire

38. Declare means the opposite of
    a. Pronounce
    b. Affirm
    c. Deny
    d. State

39. **Remark** most nearly means
   a. rebuke
   b. comment
   c. lecture
   d. replace

40. Powerful means the opposite of
   a. Commanding
   b. Insignificant
   c. Dominant
   d. Potent

41. Which word does not belong with the others?
   a. Appliance
   b. Washer
   c. Dryer
   d. Refrigerator

42. Bunch is to flowers as
   a. bale is to hay
   b. walnut is to shell
   c. cake is to party
   d. butterfly is to wing

43. Lucid means the opposite of
   a. Clear
   b. Confused
   c. Sound
   d. Logical

44. Which word does not belong with the others?
   a. Novel
   b. Short Story
   c. Autobiography
   d. Play

45. **Commence** most nearly means
   a. begin
   b. progress
   c. finish
   d. comment

46. Grapes are to wine as
   a. catsup is to French fries
   b. coffee is to cup
   c. chair is to table
   d. wheat is to bread

47. Support means the opposite of
   a. Oppose
   b. Encourage
   c. Back
   d. Aid

48. **Overdue** most nearly means
   a. overall
   b. early
   c. punctual
   d. late

49. John bought his house a month before Katherine bought hers. Ryan bought his house the same day as Katherine. John bought his house before Ryan bought his. If the first two statements are true, then the third is:
   a. True
   b. False
   c. Unknown

50. Mock is to jest as
   a. resume is to cease
   b. bowl is to cereal
   c. encompass is to surround
   d. swelter is to freeze

51. Retain means the opposite of
   a. Preserve
   b. Maintain
   c. Keep
   d. Release

52. **Solitary** most nearly means
   a. single
   b. solid
   c. sturdy
   d. stoic

53. Escalate means the opposite of
   a. Rise
   b. Soar
   c. Plummet
   d. Increase

54. **Depart** most nearly means
   a. leave
   b. describe
   c. arrive
   d. portion

55. Exercise is fitness as
    a. wing is to bird
    b. horse is to saddle
    c. laziness is to activity
    d. study is to knowledge

56. Which word does not belong with the others?
    a. English
    b. Braille
    c. French
    d. Spanish

57. **Soiled** most nearly means
    a. dirty
    b. sullen
    c. sultry
    d. dainty

58. Complete means the opposite of
    a. Finish
    b. Conclude
    c. Begin
    d. Done

59. **Puzzled** most nearly means
    a. admired
    b. retired
    c. confused
    d. understand

60. **Object** most nearly means
    a. disagree
    b. state
    c. concur
    d. relate

Reading Comprehension

The first photographs were based on the work of the German chemist Johann Heinrich Schulze who, in 1727, discovered that silver nitrate darkened upon exposure to light. The first "photograms" were images made by exposing silver nitrate on paper or metal surfaces. During the nineteenth century, a

5   number of researchers worked to combine this effect with various lenses in order to capture and reproduce images from different sources. The first process for making commercial images was ultimately announced in 1839 by Louis Jacques Mandé Daguerre, a French painter whose name became attached to the product, the daguerreotype.

10

The daguerreotype quickly became popular in Victorian England, where it was used, principally, for portraits. Today, as photography moves beyond the chemical capture of images onto paper and into the digital era, other applications abound: landscapes, interiors, sports and journalism, to name

15   but a few. And yet, the portrait remains one of the major applications for the technology.

In portraiture, as in other types of photography, the nature and characteristics of light are of the utmost importance. To the photographer,

20   light is a living thing, dynamic and animated. But, whereas in sports or journalism, for example, the photographer must make do with the light conditions he finds when it is time to shoot, light can usually be controlled for a portrait shot. And, good lighting can make all the difference in the world in a portrait, conveying mood, revealing detail, establishing the

25   photographer's style, even making a "mistake" seem like a bit of *panache.* Understanding light is the creative equivalent of a get-out-of-jail-free card. So much so that the professional portrait photographer expends a great deal of time and money on lights and equipment that will put him in charge.

30   The various lighted areas of a photograph are described as *highlights, mid-tones,* and *shadows. Specular* highlights are the brightest spots: direct reflections from the studio lights or strobes. In a portrait they are typically seen in the eyes or on the tip of the nose. From these bright portions, *diffused* highlights spread gradually into the mid-tones. At the other side of the mid-

35   tonal range, there will be *transition areas* where the available light fades gradually into the dark shadows. If these transitions are abrupt, narrow areas, the lighting is said to be *hard light.* Hard light can give a stark effect to portraits and might be used for a craggy-faced coal miner, for example, or for black-and-white shots. Broader transitions produce *soft lighting*, and lead to

40   a gentler mood. This type of lighting is more suitable for a wedding portrait, for example.

A wide variety of devices are available for producing and modifying the light in a photographic studio. Studio lighting has the advantage of being

45   reproducible, so the skilled photographer can get the same results every time. Modern lighting usually consists of flash units, also called *strobes*, rather than the

hot, power-hungry floodlights that used to be the norm. While this equipment can be elaborate and expensive, it doesn't have to be. A poor carpenter blames his tools, but with practice, one can get great results

50 from a simple setup comprised of two or three lights. Studio lighting setups vary with the preferences of the photographer, but they all have a number of elements in common.

The main light that shines on the subject is called the *key light*. The camera
55 exposure is determined by the amount of light the key throws upon the subject. The key is usually positioned off to one side of the camera, and will throw shadows across the face from the subject's nose and eyebrows. One or more *fill lights* may be used to lighten these shadowed areas and reduce image harshness. Fill lights are adjusted to throw half as much light, or less,
60 onto the subject compared to the key. A *kicker* may be positioned to illuminate the back of the model, creating a halo effect and making the subject stand out from the background. Finally, there may be *background lights* to illuminate the background directly.

65 Studio photographers often use *modifiers* of one type or another to diffuse and soften the light emanating from these sources. Modifiers make the light source effectively larger, reducing shadows and broadening transition areas. The best-known light modifier is the photographer's white umbrella, which can be used to reflect light from the source onto the model, but many other
70 types of modifiers exist. The simplest is a large piece of white cardboard, called a *fill card*. As with lights, the choice of modifiers is a matter of individual preference, and every studio photographer has his favorite combinations of lights and modifiers for achieving different effects.

75 Although the basic principles remain the same, the practice of photography has come a long way since the days of the daguerreotype.

1. The main purpose of this passage is
    a. give a history of photography
    b. to show that different photographers have different styles
    c. to compare portraiture with other forms of photography
    d. to give an overview of photographic portrait lighting

2. The main purpose of the first three paragraphs is to
    a. explain how daguerreotypes were made
    b. describe the different kinds of photography
    c. provide context for the discussion of portrait lighting
    d. contrast chemical and digital photography

3. The word "photogram" (Line 3) is between quotation marks because
    a. it is something that Johann Heinrich Schulze said.
    b. it is a coined term not in common use today.
    c. it is a German word.
    d. the author wants to place emphasis upon it.

4. The phrase "light is a living thing" (Line 20) is an example of
    a. a metaphor.
    b. a simile.
    c. an exaggeration.
    d. an anthropomorphism.

5. The word "mistake" (Line 25) is between quotation marks because
    a. it is something that someone said.
    b. it is a slang expression.
    c. it describes something that may not really be an error.
    d. all photographers make mistakes sometimes.

6. The phrase "Understanding light is the creative equivalent of a get-out-of-jail-free card" (Line 26) is an example of
    a. a metaphor.
    b. a simile.
    c. an attribution.
    d. poetic license.

7. The main purpose of paragraph 4 is to
    a. show the relationship between lighting and mood.
    b. explain the difference between hard and soft light.
    c. tell the reader what kind of lighting to use for a wedding portrait.
    d. define a number of terms used to describe lighting features on photographs.

8. The word "specular" (Line 31) is in italics because
    a. it is a term that is being defined in the sentence.
    b. it is a foreign word.
    c. it is misspelled.
    d. it is a slang expression.

9. The sentence that describes floodlights as hot and power-hungry implies that flash units, or strobes,
    a. are also hot and power-hungry.
    b. are more modern than floodlights.
    c. are more expensive than floodlights.
    d. are not hot or power-hungry.

10. The words "model" and "subject"
    a. refer to the same thing.
    b. contrast two different things that may be photographed.
    c. contrast the front and back of the person being photographed.
    d. are both conjunctions.

11. The main purpose of paragraph 6 is to
    a. describe how to set the camera exposure.
    b. tell the reader where to position a key light.
    c. define the different types of studio lights.
    d. distinguish between floodlights and strobes.

12. The main purpose of paragraph 7 is to
    a. tell the reader how to use an umbrella.
    b. explain the use of white cardboard in photography
    c. show how to make strobes brighter.
    d. describe ways to soften the light that comes from studio strobes or floodlights.

13. After reading this passage, readers should understand
    a. why portraits were popular in Victorian England.
    b. the complexity of photographic portrait lighting.
    c. why camera equipment is so expensive.
    d. exactly how to position lights for portrait photography.

Passage Two:

From 1892 to 1954, over twelve million immigrants entered the United States through the portal of Ellis Island, a small island in New York Harbor. Ellis Island is located in the upper bay just off the New Jersey coast, within the shadow of the Statue of Liberty. Through the years, this gateway to the new world was enlarged from its original 3.3 acres to 27.5 acres by landfill supposedly obtained from the ballast of ships, excess earth from the construction of the New York City subway system and elsewhere.

Before being designated as the site of one of the first Federal immigration station by President Benjamin Harrison in 1890, Ellis Island had a varied history. The local Indian tribes had called it "Kioshk" or Gull Island. Due to its rich and abundant oyster beds and plentiful and profitable shad runs, it was known as Oyster Island for many generations during the Dutch and English colonial periods. By the time Samuel Ellis became the island's private owner in the 1770's, the island had been called Kioshk, Oyster, Dyre, Bucking and Anderson's Island. In this way, Ellis Island developed from a sandy island that barely rose above the high tide mark, into a hanging site for pirates, a harbor fort, ammunition and ordinance depot named Fort Gibson, and finally into an immigration station.

14. Which of the following is true about Ellis Island?
I. It houses the Statue of Liberty.
II. The local Indian tribes called it Oyster Island.
III. It was expanded using dirt from the construction of the subway system.
    a. I only
    b. I and II only
    c. II and III only
    d. III only

15. The word "portal" in the first paragraph most likely means
    a. island.
    b. gateway.
    c. boat.
    d. subway.

16. The style of this passage is most like that found in a(n)
    a. immigrant's diary.
    b. business letter.
    c. history textbook.
    d. persuasive essay.

17. How did the island get its current name?
    a. It was named after its private owner, Samuel Ellis.
    b. It developed from a sandy island to an immigration station.
    c. It was named after its abundant oyster beds.
    d. It was an ordinance and ammunition depot.

18. The author probably included the different names of Ellis Island to show
	a. how many owners the island had.
	b. that pirates used the island.
	c. that its size was increased.
	d. the rich and varied history of the island.

Passage Three: The Coins of Ancient Greece

We don't usually think of coins as works of art, and most of them really do not invite us to do so. The study of coins, their development and history, is termed *numismatics.* Numismatics is a topic of great interest to archeologists and anthropologists, but not usually from the perspective of visual

5   delectation. The coin is intended, after all, to be a utilitarian object, not an artistic one. Many early Greek coins are aesthetically pleasing as well as utilitarian, however, and not simply because they are the earliest examples of the coin design. Rather, Greek civic individualism provides the reason. Every Greek political entity expressed its identity through its coinage.

10

The idea of stamping metal pellets of a standard weight with an identifying design had its origin on the Ionian Peninsula around 600 B.C. Each of the Greek city-states produced its own coinage adorned with its particular symbols. The designs were changed frequently to commemorate battles,

15   treaties, and other significant occasions. In addition to their primary use as a pragmatic means of facilitating commerce, Greek coins were clearly an expression of civic pride. The popularity of early coinage led to a constant demand for new designs, such that there arose a class of highly skilled artisans who took great pride in their work, so much so that they sometimes

20   even signed it. As a result, Greek coins provide us not only with an invaluable source of historical knowledge, but also with a genuine expression of the evolving Greek sense of form, as well. These minuscule works reflect the development of Greek sculpture from the sixth to the second century B.C. as dependably as do larger works made of marble or other metals. And since

25   they are stamped with the place and date of their production, they provide an historic record of artistic development that is remarkably dependable and complete.

19. What is the purpose of this passage?
    a. To attract new adherents to numismatics as a pastime.
    b. To show how ancient Greeks used coins in commerce.
    c. To teach the reader that money was invented in Greece.
    d. To describe ancient Greek coinage as an art form

20. What is meant by the phrase "most of them really do not invite us to do so", as used in the first sentence?
    a. Money is not usually included when sending an invitation.
    b. Most coins are not particularly attractive.
    c. Invitations are not generally engraved onto coins.
    d. Coins do not speak.

21. What is a synonym for "delectation", as used in the third sentence?
    a. Savoring
    b. Choosing
    c. Deciding
    d. Refusing

22. What is meant by the term numismatics (Line 3)?
    a. The study of numbers
    b. Egyptian history
    c. Greek history
    d. The study of coins

23. According to the text, how do ancient Greek coins differ from most other coinage?
    a. Simply because they were the first coins.
    b. Each political entity made its own coins.
    c. They were made of precious metals.
    d. They were designed with extraordinary care.

24. How often were new coins designed in ancient Greece?
    a. Monthly
    b. Not very often.
    c. Whenever there was a significant occasion to commemorate.
    d. When the old ones wore out.

25. What is indicated by the fact that the artisans who designed the coins sometimes signed them?
    a. They took pride in their work.
    b. They were being held accountable for their work.
    c. The signature certified the value of the coin.
    d. The Greeks had developed writing.

26. What is meant by the term pragmatic, as used in the third sentence of the second paragraph (Line 16)?
    a. Valuable
    b. Monetary
    c. Useful
    d. Practical

27. According to the passage, how are Greek coins similar to Greek sculpture?
    a. Some sculptures were made of metal.
    b. The coins were smaller.
    c. Shapes were stamped into the coins.
    d. Coin designs evolved along with the Greek sense of form.

28. Why is it significant that new coin designs were required frequently?
    a. This indicates that there was a lot of commercial activity going on.
    b. This gave the designers a lot of practice.
    c. There were a lot of things to commemorate.
    d. The Greeks needed to find new sources of precious metals.

29. Why is it significant that the coins were dated, according to the passage?
    a. The dates contributed to the designs
    b. The age of the designers could be determined.
    c. It allows historians to track the evolution of Greek artistic styles.
    d. It allows historians to know when battles and treaties took place.

30. What was the primary purpose of the Greek coin?
    a. To commemorate treaties and battles.
    b. To provide minuscule works of art.
    c. They were used as adornments.
    d. To facilitate commerce.

Passage Four: <u>Annelids</u>

    The phylum Annelida, named for the Latin word *anellus*, meaning "ring", includes earthworms, leeches, and other similar organisms. In their typical form, these animals exhibit bilateral symmetry, a cylindrical cross section, and an elongate body divided externally into segments (*metameres*) by a

5   series of rings (*annuli*). They are segmented internally as well, with most of the internal organs repeated in series in each segment. This organization is termed *metamerism*. Metameric segmentation is the distinguishing feature of this phylum, and provides it with a degree of evolutionary plasticity in that certain segments can be modified and specialized to perform specific

10   functions. For example, in some species certain of the locomotor *parapodia*, or feet, may be modified for grasping, and some portions of the gut may evolve digestive specializations.

    The gut is a straight, muscular tube that functions independently of the

15   muscular activity in the body wall. The Annelida resemble the nematodes, another worm phylum, in possessing a fluid-filled internal cavity separating the gut from the body wall. In both phyla, this cavity is involved in locomotion. However, in the annelids this space is formed at a much later time during the development of the embryo, and presumably evolved much

20   later as well. This fluid-filled internal space is called a true *coelum*.

    The annelid excretory and circulatory systems are well developed, and some members of the phylum have evolved respiratory organs. The nervous system offers a particular example of metameric specialization. It is

25   concentrated anteriorly into enlarged cerebral ganglia connected to a ventral nerve cord that extends posteriorly and is organized into repeating segmental ganglia.

    This phylum includes members bearing adaptations required for aquatic

30   (marine or freshwater) or terrestrial habitats. They may be free-living entities or exist as parasites. Among the best known are the earthworm *Lumbricus*, the water leech *Hirudo*, and the marine worm *Nereis*.

31. What is the purpose of this passage?
    a. To describe the annelid nervous system.
    b. To describe the annelid digestive system.
    c. To introduce distinctive features of annelid anatomy.
    d. To define metamerism.

32. What is meant by the term metamerism (Line 7)?
    a. Segmentation of the anatomy
    b. A series of rings
    c. Bilateral symmetry
    d. Evolutionary plasticity

33. What is meant by the term parapodia (Line 10)?
    a. Specialization
    b. Grasping appendages
    c. Locomotion
    d. Feet

34. One evolutionary advantage of segmentation is that
    a. Segmented animals have many feet.
    b. Segmented animals have a fluid-filled coelum.
    c. Parts of some segments can become specialized to perform certain functions.
    d. Segments can evolve.

35. A group of worms other than the Annelida are called
    a. Lumbricus
    b. Nematodes
    c. Leeches
    d. Parapodia

36. Some annelid feet may be specialized in order to
    a. be used for locomotion.
    b. be segmented.
    c. be fluid-filled.
    d. grasp things.

37. A difference between the annelid coelum and the fluid-filled cavity of other worms is that
    a. the annelid coelum is involved in locomotion.
    b. the annelid coelum is formed later.
    c. the annelid coelum is formed during embryology.
    d. the annelid coelum is cylindrical in cross section.

38. An example of metameric specialization in the nervous system is
    a. segmental ganglia.
    b. the ventral nerve cord.
    c. respiratory organs.
    d. cerebral ganglia

39. The main difference between the Annelida and all other animal phyla is that
    a. the Annelida are worms.
    b. the Annelida include the leeches.
    c. the Annelida are metameric.
    d. the Annelida are aquatic.

40. The purpose of the last paragraph in the passage is to
    a. give familiar examples of members of the annelid phylum.
    b. show that annelids may be parasites.
    c. tell the reader that annelids may be adapted to aquatic environments.
    d. show that there are many annelids in nature and that they are adapted to a wide variety of habitats.

41. The fluid-filled cavity in the nematodes is used for
    a. defense.
    b. reproduction.
    c. feeding.
    d. movement.

42. Members of the Annelida are
    a. free-living animals.
    b. parasites.
    c. aquatic.
    d. all the above

Reading Vocabulary Practice Questions #1

Choose the appropriate synonym for each underlined word in the following phrases:

43. He made an **oath** to his king.
    a. delivery
    b. promise
    c. statement
    d. criticism

44. Spanish is a difficult language to **comprehend**.
    a. learn
    b. speak
    c. understand
    d. appreciate

45. He **wandered** around the mall.
    a. looked
    b. shopped
    c. roamed
    d. searched

46. He is a very **courteous** young man.
    a. handsome
    b. polite
    c. inconsiderate
    d. odd

47. The child **trembled** with fear.
    a. spoke
    b. shook
    c. wept
    d. ducked

48. Her concern for him was **sincere**.
    a. intense
    b. genuine
    c. brief
    d. misunderstood

49. The math test was quite **challenging.**
    a. reasonable
    b. lengthy
    c. difficult
    d. simple

50. The audience applauded after the woman **concluded** her presentation.
    a. delivered
    b. prepared
    c. attended
    d. finished

51. The company **instantly** agreed to the terms of the contract.
    a. reluctantly
    b. eventually
    c. immediately
    d. definitely

52. The woman's **response** to the question was correct.
    a. hesitation
    b. answer
    c. decision
    d. concern

53. He **observed** the eagles with binoculars.
    a. watched
    b. hunted
    c. scared
    d. sold

54. She is having **difficulties** with her new computer.
    a. experiences
    b. solutions
    c. pleasures
    d. problems

55. The woman's performance was **superior** to the man's.
    a. short
    b. similar
    c. better
    d. weak

56. **Selecting** the best person for the job was difficult.
    a. locating
    b. contacting
    c. choosing
    d. informing

57. The fox ran **swiftly** after its prey.
    a. surely
    b. quickly
    c. slowly
    d. lightly

58. She felt intense **anguish** when her parents divorced.
    a. loneliness
    b. confusion
    c. anger
    d. sorrow

59. The class **chuckled** when the professor dropped his notes.
    a. helped
    b. commented
    c. laughed
    d. chose

60. The child was unable to **locate** his toy.
    a. buy
    b. find
    c. enjoy
    d. share

61. The bear **slumbered** in its cave.
    a. hunted
    b. fed
    c. slept
    d. explored

62. The woman **desired** a new car.
    a. purchased
    b. wanted
    c. described
    d. intended

Language
Usage, Punctuation, and Grammar
Identify the sentence that contains an error in usage, punctuation or grammar. If there are no errors, choose answer choice "d."

1.
   a. The first time I met my wife's father, I was very nervous.
   b. The grocery list contained four items; lettuce, tomatoes, cheese, and milk.
   c. John studied for his math test for three days straight.
   d. No mistake.

2.
   a. Jill graduated at the top of her class.
   b. Why does that car keep driving up and down the street?
   c. Calculus is one of the most difficult school subjects.
   d. No mistake.

3.
   a. The mountain turned out to be far higher than Jack had expected.
   b. Last June was the hottest month of the year.
   c. How long were you engaged before you got married.
   d. No mistake.

4.
   a. Seeing his daughter for the first time made John cry.
   b. There parents grounded Bill and Ben for a week.
   c. The house was not damaged in the storm, but the yard was torn up.
   d. No mistake.

5.
   a. Lesley's father doesn't understand the Internet very well.
   b. The boys were late getting to school because their car broke down.
   c. We worked on the project for day's and still got a bad grade.
   d. No mistake.

6.
   a. Bill passed his driving test on the first try.
   b. My mother always did the grocery shopping and washed the dishes after dinner.
   c. Amelia's punishment for being a bad girl was to go to bed with no dessert.
   d. No mistake.

7.
   a. Ali drove across the country all by herself last summer.
   b. The three textbooks you need is all in the bookstore.
   c. My computer crashed last night.
   d. No mistake.

8.

     a. The party was cancelled because of the rain.

     b. My house is built on seven acres of land.

     c. We went with them to the fair last year, but their not going this year.

     d. No mistake.

9.

     a. My daughter was born with a full head of hair.

     b. His car broke down for the fifth time this month.

     c. Bruce Springsteen is often thought of as one of Americas' greatest songwriters.

     d. No mistake.

10.

     a. Rocky always told people he was named after the famous movie character.

     b. Alice's favorite way to relieve her stress is to go shopping at the mall.

     c. Robin struggles with math, but she is very good at science.

     d. No mistake.

11.

     a. She ate two.

     b. The thief broke into the house through the basement window.

     c. My grandmother sold her house and moved to Florida.

     d. No mistake.

12.

     a. George Washington, and Abraham Lincoln are our two most famous leaders.

     b. The President of the United States is thought of as the leader of the free world.

     c. I went to a movie last week, but I didn't like it.

     d. No mistake.

13.

     a. The U.S. Constitution declares that all men are created equal.

     b. My father graduated from college at the top of his class.

     c. When I was in school, the Principal was a mean old woman.

     d. No mistake.

14.

     a. The last house on my street was spooky old and creepy.

     b. Jackie's mother always taught him that there were no such things as ghosts.

     c. The hardware store closed ten minutes after I got there.

     d. No mistake.

15.

     a. My sister loves cheese, but I hate it.

     b. What town did your parent's grow up in?

     c. There are three hundred sixty-five days in a year.

     d. No mistake.

16.

    a. When Sam was growing up, his family had very little money.

    b. The letter stated that my application had been denied, which was written on formal letterhead.

    c. Babe Ruth is one of the most recognized names in American sports.

    d. No mistake.

17.

    a. Bill was very nervous the first day of class; he had never been a teacher before.

    b. The yellow house across the street is much older than ours.

    c. When my brother said he was going to the movies, I said I wanted to go to.

    d. No mistake.

18.

    a. My parents didn't let me watch television when I was growing up.

    b. The movie was totally sold out; which stinks.

    c. It took me three weeks to write my term paper.

    d. No mistake.

19.

    a. The championship game was very exciting.

    b. If I come to work early tomorrow, may I leave early as well?

    c. The test had four kinds of questions: true or false, multiple choice, fill in the blank, and matching.

    d. No mistake.

20.

    a. I can always tell when Jimmy is coming to get me because his car is so loud.

    b. Steve loved playing football, baseball, and loved to run.

    c. There are not enough hours in the day for me to get all my work done.

    d. No mistake.

21.

    a. Blogging has become a very popular form of communication in the future.

    b. Richard Pryor and George Carlin were very controversial in their time.

    c. What day of the week is the party scheduled for?

    d. No mistake.

22.

    a. Most people think John was the most talented of the Beatles, but I think it was Paul.

    b. I failed the test three times before I finally passed it.

    c. War is always a controversial issue.

    d. No mistake.

23.

    a. "A mile isn't very far to run." said Steve.

    b. I learned to ride horses when I was younger.

    c. My grandmother goes to bed very early.

    d. No mistake.

24.
    a. Answering three essay questions was very difficult.
    b. Principal Walters and governor Jones had a debate on television.
    c. I like cheese and I like macaroni, but I don't like macaroni and cheese.
    d. No mistake.

25.
    a. His last business went bankrupt, so he's having a hard time getting a loan.
    b. Peyton loved the sweater her grandmother bought her.
    c. It's very comforting to know that we have such good insurance.
    d. No mistake.

26.
    a. Did you like the movie or the book better?
    b. Frank was sure he would never understand fractions.
    c. Joan forgot to turn her headlights off, so her car battery ran out.
    d. No mistake.

27.
    a. When I was in high school, I loved heavy metal music.
    b. When Sue went to the mall and bought shoes she also bought a dress and some sandals.
    c. Getting into college was much harder than Marc expected it to be.
    d. No mistake.

28.
    a. Randall were very nervous on his wedding day.
    b. The band played the fight song as the team took the court.
    c. I don't believe in the death penalty, no matter what the crime was.
    d. No mistake.

29.
    a. The team won the state championship three years in a row.
    b. Ben fell asleep on the bus and missed his stop.
    c. Two wrongs don't not make a right.
    d. No mistake.

30.
    a. If Scott and Lucy got married, they would be very happy.
    b. I went to the store, but I forgot to buy bread
    c. John is afraid of snakes, dogs, and spiders.
    d. No mistake.

31.
    a. George gets tired very easily especially when he is doing hard work.
    b. The house burned down, but no one was hurt.
    c. My daughter loves to watch I Love Lucy on television.
    d. No mistake.

32.
  a. Lesley liked to take showers at night rather than in the morning.
  b. The grocery store was completely sold out of watermelon.
  c. By the time he finished the test, Jack was exhausted.
  d. No mistake.

33.
  a. I went to the hospital to talk to the doctor on Grant Street.
  b. King Tut is the most famous of the ancient Egyptian rulers.
  c. Jackie Robinson broke baseball's color barrier.
  d. No mistake.

34.
  a. I was hoping I did well enough on the test to pass.
  b. My father was always very strict but fair.
  c. Susan asked the instructor how long the essay had to be, but he wouldn't tell her.
  d. No mistake.

35.
  a. Adam Sandler is my favorite comedian.
  b. My sister Julie always got Jerry Lewis and Jerry Lee Lewis confused.
  c. I always enjoyed reading, writing, and to sing a song.
  d. No mistake.

36.
  a. There is nothing Margie likes better than a good deep dish pizza.
  b. Her favorite subject in school was english.
  c. Will you be joining us for the trip to Miami?
  d. No mistake.

37.
  a. I love movies, and television, but I like reading better.
  b. Michael Jackson was one of the most famous musical artists of all time.
  c. The temperature was so hot, it was almost impossible to go outside.
  d. No mistake.

38.
  a. I may drink beer sometimes, but I will never drink wine.
  b. He will go to the game, but didn't stay long.
  c. We followed the road signs, but should've followed the map.
  d. No mistake.

39.
  a. I was quite scared about the results of my blood tests.
  b. If you give the dog it's bone, it might stop begging for food.
  c. What time does Mary usually get home from work?
  d. No mistake.

40.

    a. I wasn't home the night my brother came home from college.

    b. Most teachers, police officers, and fire fighters are underpaid.

    c. I've always had trouble with commas, semicolons, and hyphens.

    d. No mistake.

41.

    a. I hated going to school when I was younger.

    b. I was lazie and didn't like doing the work.

    c. As I got older, I realized that I should have worked harder.

    d. No mistake.

42.

    a. My father was a star athlete in college.

    b. I didn't like sports.

    c. My father may have been better at sports, but I got better grades.

    d. No mistake.

43.

    a. When I wreked my car, I was worried it was totaled.

    b. The mechanic said he could fix it.

    c. Even though it was very expensive, I was very relieved.

    d. No mistake.

44.

    a. The summer was very hot this year.

    b. I don't like the heat, so I was looking forward to winter.

    c. When winter came, it was so cold that I wished it was summer again.

    d. No mistake.

45.

    a. My computer stopped working in the middle of writing my essay.

    b. I was sure I had lost everything.

    c. The tecnician from computer support got it working again and saved my essay.

    d. No mistake.

46.

    a. My first aparpment was the smallest place I'd ever seen.

    b. I couldn't believe I was paying so much for so little.

    c. When I finally moved out, I was so happy.

    d. No mistake.

47.

    a. My mother ran four miles every day.

    b. She was always in great shape.

    c. When I realized how overwait I was, I started running with her.

    d. No mistake.

48.

    a. Julie believed her house was haunted.
    b. She said their were ghosts in the attic.
    c. All of her friends thought she was crazy.
    d. No mistake.

49.

    a. Television is one of the greatest inventions of all time.
    b. Before the Internet came along, television was what brought the world together.
    c. Even now, television links people together.
    d. No mistake.

50.

    a. When I graduated from college, I couldn't find a job.
    b. I thought someone would hire me right away.
    c. Eventually, I found a job, but it wasn't what I'd accepted.
    d. No mistake.

Composition Practice Questions

51. Where should the following sentence be placed in the paragraph below?

The iPad is the most popular of the new tablet computers.

1.) Experts predict that tablet computers will outsell desktop computers by 2015. 2.) Tablet computers have been gaining in popularity over the last year or so. 3.) Even the iPad though doesn't sell as well as most laptop or desktop computers. 4.) If tablet computers are going to outsell desktops, they will have to become much more popular.
   a. After sentence 1
   b. After sentence 2
   c. After sentence 3
   d. After sentence 4

52. Where should the following sentence be placed in the paragraph below?

His most famous novel is probably *The Adventures of Huckleberry Finn*.

1.) Mark Twain was one of America's greatest writers. 2.) Twain stopped writing the book for several years because he didn't know where the story would go. 3.) Most readers can tell the spot where he stopped, because the book is much different after that. 4.) The entire tone of the novel is different and it becomes a much darker story.
   a. After sentence 1
   b. After sentence 2
   c. After sentence 3
   d. After sentence 4

53. Choose the word or words that best fill the blank.

Writing, doing yoga, and _____ were her favorite activities.
   a. playing volleyball
   b. doing volleyball
   c. making volleyball
   d. volleyballing

54. Choose the word or words that best fill the blank.

Every kid in the neighborhood has _____ own bicycle.
   a. its
   b. their
   c. our
   d. her

55. Choose the word or words that best fill the blank.

A team of scientists _____ studying a new species of frog never found before.
   a. is
   b. are
   c. were
   d. have

56. Choose the sentence that is correct and most clearly written.
   a. Dr. Anderson strolled past the nurses, examining a bottle of pills.
   b. Dr. Anderson strolled past the nurses examining a bottle of pills.
   c. Dr. Anderson strolled past, the nurses examining a bottle of pills.
   d. Examining a bottle of pills, Dr. Anderson strolled past the nurses.

57. Choose the sentence that is correct and most clearly written.

Mr. King, <u>an individual of considerable influence, created a personal fortune and gave back</u> to the community.
   a. an individual of considerable influence, created a personal fortune and gave back
   b. an individual of considerable influence, he created a personal fortune and gave back
   c. an individual of considerable influence created a personal fortune and gave back
   d. an individual of considerable influence, created a personal fortune and gave it back

58. Choose the sentence that is correct and most clearly written.
   a. She is the person whose opinion matters the most.
   b. She is the person to whom opinion matters the most.
   c. She is the person who matters the most, in my opinion.
   d. She is the person for whom opinion matters the most.

59. Which sentence does not belong in the following paragraph?

1.) The New York Yankees have won more World Series championships than any other team in baseball. 2.) They have a total of twenty-seven titles. 3.) They have had some of the most famous players in history, including Babe Ruth and Mickey Mantle. 4.) The Yankees won the World Series four consecutive times from 1936 to 1939. 5.) They repeated the feat from 1949 to 1953. 6.) The Yankees won their twenty-seventh World Series title in 2009.
   a. Sentence 2
   b. Sentence 3
   c. Sentence 4
   d. Sentence 5

60. Which sentence does not belong in the following paragraph?

1.) Climate change is a very controversial topic. 2.) Many experts claim that our planet's climate is changing. 3.) These experts believe that climate change is why we experience hotter summers and warmer winters. 4.) Other experts argue that the changes in temperature are normal. 5.) Last summer, it was so hot I had to install three air conditioners in my home. 6.) Both sides have a great deal of scientific evidence to back up their claims.

    a. Sentence 2
    b. Sentence 3
    c. Sentence 4
    d. Sentence 5

Quantitative and Mathematics

Quantitative Skills

1. Put the following integers in order from greatest to least:
-52, 16, -12, 14, 8, -5, 0
  - a. -52, 16, -12, 14, 8, -5, 0
  - b. 0, -5, 8, -12, 14, 16, -52
  - c. 0, -5, -12, -52, 8, 14, 16
  - d. 16, 14, 8, 0, -5, -12, -52

2. Which of the following figures has rotational symmetry?

  a.

  b.

  c.

  d.

3. If number x is subtracted from 27, the result is -5. What is number x?
  - a. 22
  - b. 25
  - c. 32
  - d. 35

4. Which of the following letters has a vertical line of symmetry?
  - a. E
  - b. V
  - c. K
  - d. B

5. What are the first 5 multiples of 8?
  - a. 1, 2, 3, 4, 5
  - b. 0, 2, 4, 6, 8
  - c. 0, 8, 16, 24, 32
  - d. 8, 16, 24, 32, 40

6. What is 44/99 in the simplest form?
  - a. 4/9
  - b. 4/5
  - c. 11/99
  - d. 14/19

7. Which of the following fractions is halfway between 2/5 and 4/9?
   a. 2/3
   b. 2/20
   c. 17/40
   d. 19/45

8. Which of the following is the largest number?
   A. 1/2
   B. 3/8
   C. 7/16
   D. 13/54

9. Which number has no remainder when divided into 250?
   a. 5
   b. 15
   c. 20
   d. 30

10. Forty students in a class take a test that is graded on a scale of 1 to 10. The histogram in the figure shows the grade distribution, with the x-axis representing the grades and the y-axis representing the number of students obtaining each grade. If the mean, median, and modal values are represented by n, p, and q, respectively, which of the following is true?

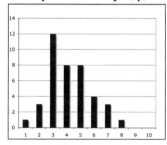

   a. $n > p > q$
   b. $n > q > p$
   c. $q > p > n$
   d. $p > q > n$

11. Equal numbers of dimes and pennies are placed in a single row on a table. Which of the following must be true?
   a. Every dime will be next to a penny.
   b. If there are two dimes at one end of the row, two pennies must be next to one another.
   c. If there is a dime at one end of the row, there must be a penny at the other end.
   d. Every penny will be between two dimes.

12. For the number set {7, 12, 5, 16, 23, 44, 18, 9, Z}, which of the following values could be equal to Z if Z is the median of the set?
   a. 14
   b. 11
   c. 12
   d. 17

13. Which of the following fractions, when entered into the triangle, makes the statement true?

$$^3/_8 < \Delta < {}^{13}/_{24}$$

    a. 7/8
    b. 5/8
    c. 5/12
    d. 1/3

14. Two even integers and one odd integer are multiplied together. Which of the following could be their product?

    a. 3.75
    b. 9
    c. 16.2
    d. 24

15. In Figure 1 (pictured below), the distance from A to D is 48. The distance from A to B is equal to the distance from B to C. If the distance from C to D is twice the distance of A to B, how far apart are B and D?

    a. 12
    b. 16
    c. 24
    d. 36

Figure 1

16. Which of the following is NOT less than .33?

    a. 4/15
    b. 13/45
    c. 26/81
    d. 4/9

17. What is the missing number in the sequence: 4, 6, 10, 18, ___, 66.

    a.   22
    b.   34
    c.   45
    d.   54

18. A garden has a perimeter of 600 yards. If the length of the garden is 250 yards, what is the garden's width?

    a.   25
    b.   50
    c.   175
    d.   350

19. Which of the following values is greatest?
    a. -4 minus 10
    b. -25 – (-30)
    c. 4(-20)
    d. -2(-10)

20. 25% of what number is 80?
    a. 200
    b. 320
    c. 160
    d. 135

21. Which algebraic expression best represents the following statement: the number of books Brian read over the summer (B) is 2 less than 3 times the number of books his brother Adam read over the summer (A)?
    a. B = 3A – 2
    b. B = 3A + 2
    c. A = 3B – 2
    d. A = 3B + 2

22. Stefan's scores on his English essays were 75, 65, 80, 95, and 65. What is the average of his test scores?
    a. 65
    b. 66
    c. 71
    d. 76

23. Which of the following is true?
    a. -(-(-4) is greater than -3
    b. -(-7) is greater than -17 minus 10
    c. -4 is greater than the absolute value of -4
    d. -10 is greater than -(-(-15)

24. Tyler is one year older than 3 times Clay's age. The sum of their ages is 21. How old is Tyler?
    a. 6
    b. 16
    c. 5
    d. 15

25. 24 is 60% of what number?
    a. 40
    b. 48
    c. 60
    d. 68

26. Jerome wants to enlarge his favorite painting by 20% (length and width). If it is currently 20 inches by 30 inches, what will the area of the enlarged painting be?
   a.   600 inches
   b.   864 inches
   c.   726 inches
   d.   926 inches

Question 27 is based on the following figure.

27. In the figure, A, B, and C are points on the number line, where O is the origin. What is the ratio of the distance *BC* to distance *AB*?
   a.   3:5
   b.   8:5
   c.   8:11
   d.   3:11

28. Arrange the following numbers in order from the least to greatest 2^3, 4^2, 6^0, 9, 10^1.
   a. 2^3, 4^2, 6^0, 9, 10^1
   b. 6^0, 9, 10^1, 2^3, 4^2
   c. 10^1, 2^3, 6^0, 9, 4^2
   d. 6^0, 2^3, 9, 10^1, 4^2

29. Dorothy is half her sister's age. She will be three fourths of her sister's age in 20 years. How many years old is she?
   a.   10
   b.   15
   c.   20
   d.   25

30. *Use the figure below to answer question.*

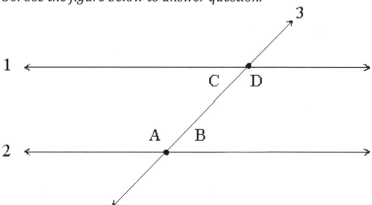

Which of the following statements is true about the figure above?
    a.   Lines 1 and 2 are parallel.
    b.   Lines 1 and 3 are parallel.
    c.   Lines 1 and 2 intersect.
    d.   Line 1 bisects line 3.

31. 30% of 50 equals 50% of what number?
    a.   30
    b.   25
    c.   20
    d.   15

32. If the average of 7 and x is equal to the average of 9, 4, and x, what is the value of x?
    a.   4
    b.   5
    c.   6
    d.   7

33. If four friends had an average score of 92 on a test, what was Annie's score if Bill got an 86, Clive got a 98 and Demetrius got a 90?
    a.   88
    b.   90
    c.   92
    d.   94

34. If one side of a square has a length of 56 cm, what is its perimeter?
    a.   112 cm
    b.   224 cm
    c.   448 cm
    d.   3136 cm

35. Four people decide to adopt a dog and take turns caring for it. Person A thinks he can take care of the dog 1/4 of the time; person B thinks she can handle 1/8; person C thinks he can take care of the dog 1/2 of the time. What part of the fourth person's time will have to be spent caring for the dog?
   A. 1/8
   B. 1/4
   C. 1/3
   D. 1/2

36. A skyscraper is 548 meters high. The building's owners decide to increase its height by 3%. How high would the skyscraper be after the increase?
   a. 551 meters
   b. 555 meters
   c. 562 meters
   d. 564 meters

37. If a rectangle's length and width are doubled, by what percentage does its area increase?
   a. 20
   b. 80
   c. 160
   d. 300

38. If the value of ABC Corporation stock rises from $31 per share to $35 per share, what is the approximate percent of the increase?
   a. 16
   b. 12.9
   c. 6.9
   d. 26

39. Which of the following is greatest?
   a. 4/5 of 80
   b. 20% of 20
   c. 7% of 1,400
   d. 32 + 4

40. The average of six numbers is 4. If the average of two of those numbers is 2, what is the average of the other four numbers?
   a. 5
   b. 6
   c. 7
   d. 8

41. What is the next-highest prime number after 67?
   a. 68
   b. 69
   c. 71
   d. 73

42. How many 3-inch segments can a 4.5-yard line be divided into?
   a.   15
   b.   45
   c.   54
   d.   64

43. $4^6 \div 2^8 =$
   a.   2
   b.   8
   c.   16
   d.   32

44. Archie's gas tank is 1/3 full. If Archie adds 3 gallons of gas to the tank, it will be ½ full. What is the capacity in gallons of Archie's tank?
   a.   28
   b.   12
   c.   20
   d.   18

45. If 12 is added to the product of 13 and 7, the result is
   a.   32
   b.   79
   c.   103
   d.   240

46. Which of the following is a multiple of 3, 4, and 5?
   a.   120
   b.   150
   c.   170
   d.   190

47. What is the mode of the following numbers: 14, 17, 14, 12, 13, 15, 22, 11?
   a.   13.5
   b.   14
   c.   14.75
   d.   16.5

48. What is 65 increased by 33%?
   a.   21.45
   b.   33.25
   c.   75.65
   d.   86.45

49. $2(7 + 8)^2 - 12\ (6 \times 2) =$
   a.   119
   b.   225
   c.   306
   d.   604

50. Which of the following numbers is greatest?
    a. 0.0236
    b. 0.236
    c. 0.0339
    d. 0.099

51. What is 2.34 x 10^6 written in standard notation?
    a. 0.000234
    b. 23,400
    c. 234,000
    d. 2,340,000

52. What is the value of -9 - (-8)?
    a. -1
    b. -17
    c. 1
    d. 17

Mathematics

1. There are n musicians in a marching band. All play either a drum or a brass instrument. If p represents the fraction of musicians playing drums, how many play a brass instrument?
    a. $pn-1$
    b. $p(n-1)$
    c. $(p-1)n$
    d. $(1-p)n$

2. Which of the following can be divided by 3, with no remainder?
    a.   2018
    b.   46
    c.   8912
    d.   555

3. A bullet travels at 5×10^6 feet per hour. If it strikes its target in 2×10^{-4} hours, how far has it traveled?
    a.   50 feet
    b.   25 feet
    c.   100 feet
    d.   1000 feet

4. A blouse normally sells for $138, but is on sale for 25% off. What is the cost of the blouse?
    a. $67
    b. $103.50
    c. $34.50
    d. $113

5. Which number equals 2^{-3}?
    a.   ½
    b.   ¼
    c.   1/8
    d.   1/16

6. What is the surface area, in square inches, of a cube if the length of one side is 3 inches?
    a.   9
    b.   27
    c.   54
    d.   18

7. Which of the following values is closest to the diameter of a circle with an area of 314 square inches?
    a.   20 inches
    b.   10 inches
    c.   100 inches
    d.   31.4 inches

8. The following table shows the distance from a point to a moving car at various times.

d	Distance	50	70	110
t	Time	2	3	5

If the speed of the car is constant, which of the following equations describes the distance from the point to the car?
   a. $d = 25\,t$
   b. $d = 35\,t$
   c. $d = 55\,t$
   d. $d = 20\,t + 10$

9. A circle has a perimeter of 35 feet. What is its diameter?
   a. 11.14 feet
   b. 6.28 feet
   c. 5.57 feet
   d. 3.5 feet

Question 10 is based upon the following table:

English-Metric Equivalents	
1 meter	1.094 yard
2.54 centimeter	1 inch
1 kilogram	2.205 pound
1 liter	1.06 quart

10. A sailboat is 19 meters long. What is its length in inches?
   a. 254
   b. 1094
   c. 4826
   d. 748

11. A metal rod used in manufacturing must be as close a possible to 15 inches in length. The tolerance of the length, L, in inches, is specified by the inequality $|L - 15| \le 0.01$. What is the minimum length permissible for the rod?
   a. 14.9 inches
   b. 14.99 inches
   c. 15.01 inches
   d. 15.1 inches

12. Two numbers are said to be reciprocal if their product equals 1. Which of the following represents the reciprocal of the variable x ?
   a. $x - 1$
   b. $\dfrac{1}{x}$
   c. x^{-1}
   d. Both B and C.

13. Which of the following expressions is equivalent to the equation $3x^2 + 4x - 15$?
    a. $(x-3)(x+5)$
    b. $(x+5)(3+x^2)$
    c. $x(3x+4-15)$
    d. $(x+3)(3x-5)$

14. Prizes are to be awarded to the best pupils in each class of an elementary school. The number of students in each grade is shown in the table, and the school principal wants the number of prizes awarded in each grade to be proportional to the number of students. If there are twenty prizes, how many should go to fifth grade students?

Grade	1	2	3	4	5
Students	35	38	38	33	36

    a. 5
    b. 4
    c. 7
    d. 3

15. Which of the following expressions is equivalent to $3(\dfrac{6x-3}{3}) - 3(9x+9)$?

    a. A. $-3(7x+10)$
    b. -3x +6
    c. C. $(x+3)(x-3)$
    d. D. $3x^2 - 9$

16. Evaluate the expression $(x-2y)^2$ where x = 3 and y = 2.
    a. -1
    b. +1
    c. +4
    d. -2

17. Which of the following expressions is equivalent to $(3x^{-2})^3$?
    a. $9x^{-6}$
    b. $9x^{-8}$
    c. $27x^{-8}$
    d. $27x^{-4}$

18. To determine a student's grade, a teacher throws out the lowest grade obtained on 5 tests, averages the remaining grades, and round up to the nearest integer. If Betty scored 72, 75, 88, 86, and 90 on her tests, what grade will she receive?
    a. 68
    b. 85
    c. 88
    d. 84.8

19. There is a big sale on at the clothing store on Main Street. Everything is marked down by 33% from the original price, p. Which of the following expressions describes the sale price, S, to be paid for any item?

    a. $S = p - 0.33$
    b. $S = p - 0.33p$
    c. $S = 0.33p$
    d. $S = 0.33(1 - p)$

20. The town of Fram will build a water storage tank on a hill overlooking the town. The tank will be a right circular cylinder of radius R and height H. The plot of ground selected for the installation is large enough to accommodate a circular tank 60 feet in diameter. The planning commission wants the tank to hold 1,000,000 cubic feet of water, and they intend to use the full area available. Which of the following is the minimum acceptable height?

    a. 655 ft
    b. 455 ft
    c. 355 ft
    d. 255 ft

21. Given the equation $\dfrac{3}{y-5} = \dfrac{15}{y+4}$, what is the value of y?

    a. 45
    b. 54
    c. $\dfrac{29}{4}$
    d. $\dfrac{4}{29}$

22. The weight in pounds of five students is 112, 112, 116, 133, 145. What is the median weight of the group?

    a. 123.6
    b. 116
    c. 112
    d. 118.5

23. Which of the following expressions is equivalent to *(a)(a)(a)(a)(a)* for all values of *a*, positive or negative?

    a. $5a$
    b. a^{-5}
    c. $a^{-\frac{1}{5}}$
    d. a^{5}

24. How many real-number solutions exist for the equation $x^2 + 1 = 0$?
   a. 0
   b. 1
   c. 2
   d. 3

25. Rachel spent $24.15 on vegetables. She bought 2 lbs of onions, 3 lbs of carrots, and 1 ½ lbs of mushrooms. If the onions cost $3.69 per lb, and the carrots cost $ 4.29 per lb, what is the price per lb of mushrooms?
   a. $2.60
   b. $2.25
   c. $2.80
   d. $3.10

Question 26 is based on the following figure.

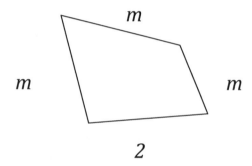

26. The figure shows an irregular quadrilateral and the lengths of its individual sides. Which of the following equations best represents the perimeter of the quadrilateral?
   a. $m^4 + 5$
   b. $2m^4 + 5$
   c. $4m + 5$
   d. $5m + 5$

27. Elijah drove 45 miles to his job in an hour and ten minutes in the morning. On the way home: however, traffic was much heavier and the same trip took an hour and a half. What was his average speed in miles per hour for the round trip?
   a. 30
   b. 45
   c. 33 ¾
   d. 32 ½

28. Which of the following is a solution to the inequality $4x-12<4$?
   a. 4
   b. 6
   c. 5
   d. 3

29. If a = -6 and b = 7, then $4a(3b+5)+2b=$?
   a. 638
   b. 624
   c. 610
   d. -610

30. An airplane leaves Atlanta at 2 PM and flies north at 250 miles per hour. A second airplane leaves Atlanta 30 minutes later and flies north at 280 miles per hour. At what time will the second airplane overtake the first?
   a. 6:00 PM
   b. 6:20 PM
   c. 6:40 PM
   d. 6:50 PM

31. Which of the following expressions is equivalent to x^3x^5?
   a. $2x^8$
   b. x^{15}
   c. x^2
   d. x^8

32. If $\dfrac{12}{x}=\dfrac{30}{6}$, what is the value of x?
   a. 3.6
   b. 2.4
   c. 3.0
   d. 2.0

Question 33 is based on the following table.

Hours	1	2	3
Cost	$3.60	$7.20	$10.80

33. The table shows the cost of renting a bicycle for 1,2, or 3 hours. Which of the following equations best represents the data, if C represents the cost and h represents the time of the rental?
   a. $C=3.60h$
   b. $C=h+3.60$
   c. $C=3.60h+10.80$
   d. $C=10.80/h$

34. Rafael has a business selling computers. He buys computers from the manufacturer for $450 each and sells them for $800. Each month, he must also pay fixed costs of $3000 for rent and utilities at his store. If he sells n computers in a month, which of the following equations can be used to calculate his profit?

    a. $P = n(800 - 450)$
    b. $P = n(800 - 450 - 3000)$
    c. $P = 3000n(800 - 450)$
    d. $P = n(800 - 450) - 3000$

35. Arrange the following numbers in order from the least to greatest $2^3, 4^2, 6^0, 9, 10^1$.

    A. $2^3, 4^2, 6^0, 9, 10^1$
    B. $6^0, 9, 10^1, 2^3, 4^2$
    C. $10^1, 2^3, 6^0, 9, 4^2$
    D. $6^0, 2^3, 9, 10^1, 4^2$

Question 36 is based on the following diagram:

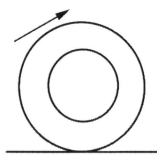

36. A tire on a car rotates at 500 RPM (revolutions per minute) when the car is traveling at 50 km/hr (kilometers per hour). What is the circumference of the tire, in meters?

    a. $\dfrac{50,000}{2\pi}$

    b. $\dfrac{50,000}{60 \times 2\pi}$

    c. $\dfrac{50,000}{500 \times 2\pi}$

    d. $\dfrac{10}{6}$

37. Which of the following expressions is equivalent to $(a + b)(a - b)$?

    a. $a^2 - b^2$
    b. $(a + b)^2$
    c. $(a - b)^2$
    d. $ab(a - b)$

38. Which of the following expressions represents the ratio of the area of a circle to its circumference?

a. πr^2

b. $\dfrac{\pi r^2}{2\pi}$

c. $\dfrac{2\pi r}{r^2}$

d. $\dfrac{r}{2}$

39. Which of the following are complementary angles?

a. 71° and 19°
b. 18° and 18°
c. 90° and 90°
d. 90° and 45°

40. What is the value of r in the following equation?
$29 + r = 420$

a. $r = 29/420$
b. $r = 420/29$
c. $r = 391$
d. $r = 449$

41. If 35% of a paycheck was deducted for taxes and 4% for insurance, what is the total percent taken out of the paycheck?

a. 20%
b. 31%
c. 39%
d. 42%

42. In the year 2000, 35% of the company sales were in electronics. The table below shows how electronic sales have changed for the company over the years. Find the percent of electronics sold in 2005.

Years	Change
2000 - 2001	-2
2001 - 2002	-1
2002 - 2003	+6
2003 - 2004	-1
2004 - 2005	+2

a. 2%
b. 11%
c. 39%
d. 42%

- 128 -

43. Which of the following choices expresses 5/8 as a percent?
    a. 40%
    b. 58%
    c. 62.5%
    d. 65%

44. In the following figure, angle b = 120°. What is the measurement of angle a?

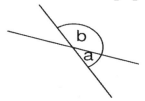

    a. 40°
    b. 60°
    c. 90°
    d. 100°

45. A woman wants to stack two small bookcases beneath a window that is 26½ inches from the floor. The larger bookcase is 14½ inches tall. The other bookcase is 8¾ inches tall. How tall with the two bookcases be when they are stacked together?
    a. 12 inches tall
    b. 23¼ inches tall
    c. 35¼ inches tall
    d. 41 inches tall

46. A man has $1000. He adds 10% to the total amount of money. Then he takes away 10% of the total amount. How much money does he have now?
    a. $800
    b. $900
    c. $990
    d. $1000

47. Solve for y in the following equation if x = -3
$y = x + 5$
    a. $y = -2$
    b. $y = 2$
    c. $y = 3$
    d. $y = 8$

48. Which of the following is the symbol that represents the negative square root of 100?
   a. $\sqrt{-100}$

   b. $\sqrt{100}$

   c. $\sqrt{10}$

   d. $-\sqrt{100}$

49. What is the simplest way to write the following expression?
5x – 2y + 4x + y
   a. $9x - y$
   b. $9x - 3y$
   c. $9x + 3y$
   d. $x ; y$

50. Find the sum.
$(3x^2 + x + 3) + 8x^2 + 5x + 16$
   a. $7x^2 + 29\ x^2$
   b. $11x^2 + 6x + 19$
   c. $30x + 19$
   d. $(3x^2 + 3x) + 13x^2 + 16$

51. Angle AEC is a straight line. Angle BEC is 45°. What is the measure for angle AEB?

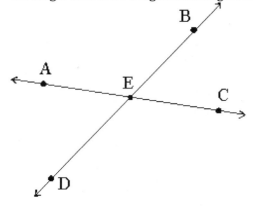

   a. Angle AEB is 90°
   b. Angle AEB is 115°
   c. Angle AEB is 135°
   d. Angle AEB is 180°

52. A pasta salad was chilled in the refrigerator at 35° F overnight for 9 hours. The temperature of the pasta dish dropped from 86° F to 38° F. What was the average rate of cooling per hour?
   a. 4.8°/hr
   b. 5.3°/hr
   c. 5.15°/hr
   d.   0.532°/hr

53. What is the missing number in the sequence: 4, 6, 10, 18, __, 66.
   a. 22
   b. 34
   c. 45
   d. 54

54. What is $(x^2)^3 \cdot (y^2)^5 \cdot (y^4)^3$?
   a. $x^6 y^{22}$
   b. $x^6 y^{120}$
   c. $x^5 y^{14}$
   d. $x^6 y^{-2}$

55. Simplify the following fraction: $[(x^2)^5 y^6 z^2] \, / \, [x^4 (y^3)^4 z^2]$.
   a. $x^{40} y^{72} z^4$
   b. $x^6 y^{-6}$
   c. $x^3 y^{-1}$
   d. $x^{14} y^{18} z^4$

56. There are 64 fluid ounces in a ½ gallon. If Nora fills a tank that holds 8 ¾ gallons, how many ounces will she use?
   a. 560 ounces
   b. 1,024 ounces
   c. 1,088 ounces
   d. 1,120 ounces

57. A house is 25 feet tall and a ladder is set up 35 feet away from the side of the house. Approximately how long is the ladder from the ground to the roof of the house?
   a. 43 ft
   b. 25 ft
   c. 50 ft
   d. 62 ft

58. On a map, the space of ½ of an inch represents 15 miles. If two cities are 4 3/5 inches apart on the map, what is the actual distance between the two cities?
   a. 138 miles
   b. 39 miles
   c. 23 miles
   d. 125 miles

59. A soda company is testing a new sized can to put on the market. The new can is 6 inches in diameter and 12 inches in height. What is the volume of the can in cubic inches?
   a. 339
   b. 113
   c. 432
   d. 226

60. A garden has a perimeter of 600 yards. If the length of the garden is 250 yards, what is the garden's width?
   a. 25
   b. 50
   c. 175
   d. 350

61. A farmer set up a rain gauge in his field and recorded the following daily precipitation amounts over the course of a week: 0.45 inches, 0.0 inches, 0.75 inches, 1.20 inches, 1.1 inches, 0.2 inches, and 0.0 inches. What was the average precipitation over that week?
   a. 0.74 in
   b. 1.05 in
   c. 0.53 in
   d. 3.70 in

62. While at the airport, Adrienne shops for perfume because the product is duty-free, meaning there is no sales tax. If she makes a purchase of $55.00 and the sales tax in that city is 7%, how much money has she saved?
   a. $3.85
   b. $0.38
   c. $7.85
   d. $4.65

63. Enrique is a full-time employee who earns $12.00 per hour. If he works overtime, he receives time-and-a-half (where each hour worked over 40 hours is compensated at 1.5 times the regular rate). If Enrique works 45 hours, how much money will he earn?
   a. $540
   b. $570
   c. $510
   d. $600

64. How many feet are in 5 1/3 yards?
   a. 15
   b. 1 7/9
   c. 15 1/3
   d. 16

Answers and Explanations

Verbal Skills

1. A: When it is said that someone is generous, it usually means they are giving and unselfish.

2. A: An elevator is part of a building as a seat is part of a theater. (B) and (C) both contain parts of larger items, but the order is reversed.

3. A: Significant means meaningful, which is the opposite of trivial.

4. D: Furniture is the category to which the other answers belong.

5. C: Unknown
The first sentence can be diagrammed as follows: Lesley > Steve. But it is unclear from the second sentence whether Steve is older or younger than Barb. Therefore, it is impossible to tell if Lesley is older or younger than Barb.

6. C: Valuable means important, which is the opposite of worthless.

7. B: Man is the opposite of the other three words, which are all synonyms.

8. D: Coarse, which means rough or composed of relatively large parts, is the opposite of fine, which means polished or composed of tiny parts. In (D), deliberate is the opposite of accidental. (A) and (B) represent synonyms, not antonyms. (C) represents a person and a state of being.

9. A: A residence is a place where a person lives; the term is often used to refer to someone's home.

10. B: False
The first two sentences can be diagrammed as follows: Monica > Ray > Juliet. Sentence three, Juliet > Monica, is inconsistent with the first two sentences. It is false.

11. B: Annoying means causing irritation, which is the opposite of pleasing.

12. D: The other three words are all types of domiciles.

13. D: Flagrant means overt, which is the opposite of obscure.

14. C: Something that is described as gigantic is extremely large, or huge, in size.

15. D: One may move across ice by skating as one may move through water by swimming. (C) does not involve mobility.

16. A: Righteous means good, which is the opposite of evil.

17. A: True
The first two sentences can be diagrammed as follows: Rocco > Ashley > Brian. Sentence three, Rocco > Brian, is consistent with the first two sentences. It is true.

18. B: Flat means without any bumps or curves, which is the opposite of uneven.

19. D: An opportunity is a chance to do something. For example, saying someone was given the *opportunity* to go to school or saying somebody was given the *chance* to go to school conveys the same meaning.

20. D: Global means comprehensive or wide ranging, which is the opposite of narrow.

21. D: A driver steers a truck as an engineer steers a train. (A) contains this relationship but in the opposite order.

22. C: Unknown
The first two sentences can be diagrammed as follows: Bill > Stan and Randall > Stan. It is impossible to tell from the information provided if Randall > Bill.

23. C: The other answers are all types of dogs, while a cardinal is a type of bird.

24. A: Morose means miserable, which is the opposite of upbeat.

25. C: Oblivious means unaware, which is the opposite of conscious.

26. C: To say that something is done frequently implies that it is done regularly or often.

27. A: True
The first two sentences can be diagrammed as follows: Reece > Scott > Della. Sentence three, Reece > Della, is consistent with the first two sentences. It is true.

28. D: An extreme form of snow is an avalanche as an extreme form of wind is an element of a tornado. (C) may be a tempting answer, but a river is a commonplace rather than extreme form of water, and therefore, not the best answer.

29. D: Compact means solid, which is the opposite of loose.

30. B: False
The first two sentences can be diagrammed as follows: Monday > Thursday > Tuesday. Sentence three, Thursday > Monday, is inconsistent with the first two sentences. It is false.
31. D: Saying that somebody purchased something and saying they bought something conveys the same meaning.

32. B: Almost means approximately, which is the opposite of exactly.

33. B: Crying is an expression of sadness as yelling is an expression of anger. (C) contains this relationship but in the wrong order.

34. A: Change means modify, which is the opposite of remain.

- *134* -

35. A: When it is said that something is entire, it usually means that it is still whole. For example, if someone says they ate an entire apple, it is the same as saying they ate a whole apple.

36. B: False
The first two sentences can be diagrammed as follows: Soccer > football > baseball. Sentence three, baseball > soccer, is inconsistent with the first two sentences. It is false.

37. C: Water quenches thirst as food quenches hunger. The other answers do not reflect this relationship.

38. A: Declare means assert, which is the opposite of deny.

39. B: A remark is a spoken statement, also commonly known as a comment. To say somebody made a remark conveys the same meaning as saying they made a comment.

40. B: Powerful means great, which is the opposite of insignificant.

41. A: Appliance is the category to which the other answers belong.

42. A: Flowers are gathered together in a bunch as hay is gathered together in a bale. The other answers do not reflect this collective notion.

43. B: Lucid means coherent, which is the opposite of confused.

44. C: The other three answers are works of fiction. Autobiographies are nonfiction.

45. A: To commence something is to begin or start something.

46. D: Grapes are an ingredient of wine as wheat is an ingredient of bread. The other answers do not reflect this relationship.

47. A: Support means help, which is the opposite of oppose.

48 D: When something is overdue, it means that it is late. For example, when a bill is overdue, it means that it has not been paid on time.

49. A: True
The first two sentences can be diagrammed as follows: John > Katherine = Ryan. Sentence three, John > Ryan, is consistent with the first two sentences. It is true.

50. C: Mock is a synonym of jest. In (C), encompass is a synonym of surround. (A) and (D) are antonyms. (B) does not represent synonymous relationships.

51. D: Retain means to hold onto, which is the opposite of release.

52. A: Solitary can mean a number of different things, but one meaning is single. For example, if you said there was a solitary tree in a yard, you would mean that there was a single tree.

53. C: Escalate means rise, which is the opposite of plummet.

54. A: If somebody or something is departing from somewhere, it means they are leaving. For example, to say the train departed from the station is the same as saying the train left the station.

55. D: Exercise causes fitness as study causes knowledge. The other answers do not represent this causal relationship.

56. B: The other answers are all spoken languages. Braille is not a language; rather, it is a technique that enables blind and visually impaired people to read and write.

57. A: Something that is soiled is stained or dirty. When somebody says their clothing is soiled, it is the same as saying their clothing is dirty.

58. C: Complete means finish, which is the opposite of begin.

59. C: If somebody is puzzled about something, it implies confusion or bewilderment. For example, to say that a man was puzzled by the woman's reaction means that the man was confused by her reaction.

60. A: When somebody objects to something, it means that they disagree with it. A person who objects to the expression of a specific political opinion may be said to disagree with it.

Reading Comprehension

1. D: After introducing its topic, the bulk of the passage describes the features that light produces on a photograph and the kinds of lighting that are used to produce these features.

2. C: The paragraphs describe the origins of photography and the early popularity of the portrait, then sets the stage for the description of lighting methods by indicating the importance of good lighting for the portrait.

3. B: The quotation marks are used to show that the word was invented to describe the results of Schulze's process, but was later replaced by other terms to describe the outputs of photographic methods, and is no longer in use.

4. A: Light is being compared to a living thing, with characteristics of dynamism and animation, explicitly stating that a comparison is being made. (Light IS a living thing.) This is the definition of a metaphor, as opposed to a simile, in which the comparison shows two things to be similar, usually through the use of the preposition "like" or "as." (Light IS LIKE a living thing.)

5. C: The word is used here to describe something a photographer may do that is different from common methods, but that may be an element of his or her personal style. The point is that by showing technical competence with good lighting technique, the "mistake" may be presented as a deliberate flaunting of convention.

6. A: By using the noun "equivalent" to characterize the comparison, the author makes it explicit. Thus, it is a metaphor and not a simile. A simile is similar ("like" or "as") but not exact.

7. D: While all the other choices describe information that is included in the paragraph, its main purpose is to define a large number of terms.

8. A: The author uses this technique throughout the passage: placing a term in italics and using it in a sentence that describes what it means.

9. D: The sentence contrasts floodlights with strobes and implies that strobes, being more modern, do not share these negative characteristics of floodlights.

10. A: Both words refer to the person being photographed. The author uses them in this manner to avoid repeating the same word twice in one sentence.

11. C: The paragraph runs through the different kinds of lights used for portraiture, presenting the name of each in italics and in a sentence that describes or defines it.

12. D: The paragraph describes several ways of modifying the output of studio lights to "diffuse and soften" their output.

13. B: The passage describes the different types of studio portrait lights, modifiers, and the lighting features that they produce on a photograph. It does not go into detail on positioning (Choice D).

14. D: The only true statement about Ellis Island is statement III: The island was expanded using dirt excavated from the construction of the New York City subway system. Statement I is false. According to Paragraph 1, Ellis Island is "within the shadow" of the Statue of

Liberty. This means that it is close to the Statue of Liberty, but does not house the Statue of Liberty. Statement II is also false. Paragraph 2 states that the local Indian tribes had called it "Kioshk" or Gull Island, not Oyster Island.

15. B: To correctly answer this question, reread the sentence, replacing "portal" with each of the answer choices:

An island is a piece of land completely surrounded by water. This word does not make sense in the sentence.

A gateway is a passage or point where a region may be entered. This choice makes the most sense in the sentence and can replace the word "portal". This is the correct answer choice.
A boat is a vessel used to travel in water. This word does not make sense in the sentence.
A subway is an underground railway used in a large city. This word does not make sense in the sentence.

16. C: The author's style is giving facts and details, much like the style used in a history textbook. An immigrant's diary would be written in first-person and most likely give thoughts and feelings about the experience at Ellis Island. A business letter would have a date, salutation, and closing. A persuasive essay would use persuasive techniques to persuade the reader to adopt a particular argument or position, and a short story would be written to entertain, not inform.

17. A: Throughout its history, the island had different many names. To answer this question, first determine the current name of the island. The first sentence of the passage states the current name of the island, Ellis Island. You can infer from Paragraph 2 that the island's current name came from the name of a private owner, Samuel Ellis. All the other answer choices are true statements from the passage, but do not make a correct inference about the current name of the island.

18. D: The author most likely included all the names of the island to demonstrate to the reader the rich and varied history of Ellis Island. The author states that "Ellis Island had a varied history," just before listing and explaining the various names the island had throughout its history.

19. D: The passage describes the artistry of Greek coinage and gives the reasons why so much effort went into designing them.

20. B: The first sentence shows that the author thinks of coins as utilitarian objects and that few of them are designed in a manner that makes them worth considering as something more than that.

21. A: "Delectation" means to savor or to enjoy the flavor or beauty of something, in this case the design of the coins.

22. D: The word is defined in passing in the text in the second sentence.

23. D: The passage describes the coins as artistic objects, not simply because they were the first coins, but also because of the historical situation which is described, and which led to their being designed with great care and pride.

24. C: The text states that new coins were developed frequently, to commemorate battles, treaties, etc.

25. A: The text tells us that the designers were highly skilled and that they were so proud of their work that they signed it.

26. D: The sentence contrasts the artistic content of the coins with their use as a practical means of commercial exchange.

27. D: The text tells us that coin designs changed along with larger sculptures to reflect changing Greek artistic tastes.

28. B: The frequent need for new designs meant that the artisans who did the work had ample opportunity to perfect their skills.

29. C: The text tells us that the dated coins provide a dependable record of Greek artistic development.

30. D.
Coins were developed as a means of commercial exchange, and the text tells us that this was their main use.

31. C: The passage describes several distinctive features of annelid anatomy and tells how some of them differ from other worms.

32. A: The term is defined in the text as an organization of the anatomy into segments.

33. D: The term is defined in the text between commas.

34. C: The text gives the example of feet specializing into grasping organs to illustrate this evolutionary advantage of segmental plasticity.

35. B: *Nematodes* differ from the annelids in the structure of the coelum. *Lumbricus* and leeches are both members of the Annelida.

36. D: The text gives the example of parapodia modified for grasping to illustrate evolutionary plasticity among metameres.

37. B: The text states that the annelid coelum is formed later during embryology and probably evolved at a later time, as well.

38. D: The text indicates that the cerebral ganglia are enlarged, whereas the remaining ganglia in the nerve cord are merely repeating (unspecialized) units.

39. C: The text defines metemeres as segments, and discusses segmentation as the distinguishing feature of the phylum.

40. D: The paragraph tells us that annelids can live in salt or fresh water and on land, and then gives examples.

41. D: The text indicates that both nematodes and annelids possess a fluid-filled cavity which is involved in locomotion, or movement.

42. D: The last paragraph indicates that annelids occupy all the habitats listed and gives examples.

43. B: An oath is a promise. For example, if you make an oath to keep a secret, you are promising to keep that secret.

44. C: If you say that you comprehend something, it is the same as saying you understand it. For example, saying you comprehend what another person is saying is the same as saying you understand them.

45. C: To wander is to roam. To say someone wandered around a mall is to say they roamed or walked around aimlessly, without a specific goal or destination in mind.

46. B: Describing somebody as courteous implies that they are polite and well-mannered. Polite and courteous both convey the same meaning.

47. B: Tremble is another word for shake. To say somebody or something trembled means that it shook or shuddered.

48. B: To say something is sincere means that it is genuine or real. For example, saying someone showed sincere concern means that their concern was genuine, and not fake.

49. C: When something is described as challenging, it usually means that it is difficult or demanding.
50. D: When something is concluded, it means that it is finished or completed.

51. C: To say something was done instantly means that it was done immediately and without hesitation.

52. B: A response is also commonly known as an answer. A response to a question carries the same meaning as an answer to a question.

53. A: Something that is being observed is being watched. Binoculars are used to see things more clearly, so it makes sense that the man would be observing or watching eagles with binoculars.

54. D: The word difficulty implies hardship. When it is said that somebody is having difficulties with another person or thing, it usually means they are experiencing problems.

55. C: To say something is superior to something else usually implies that it is better.

56. C: When a selection is being made, it involves making a choice between several options. Selecting something is the same as choosing something.

57. B: When something is done swiftly, it means that it is done fast or quickly.

58. D: Somebody who is experiencing or feeling anguish is experiencing sorrow or sadness.

59. C: Chuckled is a synonym for laughed. To say somebody chuckled or to say that somebody laughed conveys the same meaning.

60. B: To locate something that is lost or misplaced is to find it. For example, the child could not locate (find) his toy.

61. C: Slumber is another word for sleep. Saying someone slumbered is the same as saying they slept.

62. B: To desire something is to want something. Saying that a woman desired a new car has the same meaning as saying the woman wanted a new car.

Language

Usage, Punctuation, and Grammar

1. B: The grocery list had four items on it; lettuce, tomatoes, cheese, and milk.
Error: semicolon
The semicolon between "items" and "lettuce" is incorrect. A colon should be used before a list.

2. D: No mistake.

3. C: How long were you engaged before you got married.
Error: period
The period at the end of the sentence is incorrect. The sentence is a question; therefore, it needs a question mark at the end.

4. B: There parents grounded Bill and Ben for a week.
Error: Incorrect word choice. Although "there" and "their" are pronounced the same way, the two words have different meanings. "There" is a location. "Their" is the possessive form of the pronoun "they" and it is the correct word to use in this sentence.

5. C: We worked on the project for day's and still got a bad grade.
Error: apostrophe
An apostrophe makes a word possessive, not plural. The proper form of the word in this case is "days."

6. D: No mistake.

7. B: The three textbooks you need is all in the bookstore.

8. C: We went with them to the fair last year, but their not going this year.
Error: Incorrect word choice. Although "their" and "they're" are pronounced the same way, the two words have different meanings. "Their" is the possessive form of the pronoun "they". "They're" is a contraction of they words "they are" and it is the correct word to use in this sentence.

9. C: Bruce Springsteen is often thought of as one of Americas' greatest songwriters.
Error: apostrophe
The apostrophe should go between the "a" and the "s" in America's. America is a collective noun, which means that it refers to a group of people, places or things. In the United States, the singular form of a verb is commonly used for a collective noun.

10. D: No mistake.

11. A: She ate two.
Error: sentence fragment
The sentence is incomplete. To be a complete thought, it would need to include what she ate two of. For example, "She ate two burgers" would be a complete sentence.

12. A: George Washington, and Abraham Lincoln are our two most famous leaders.
Error: comma
There should not be a comma between "Washington" and "and". There are only two items in the list; therefore, a comma is unnecessary.

13. C: When I was in school, the Principal was a mean old woman.
Error: capitalization
Principal should be capitalized only when used as part of a name, such as in Principal Skinner.

14. A: The last house on my street was spooky old and creepy.
Error: commas
The list of adjectives describing the house needs to be divided by commas: "The last house on my street was spooky, old, and creepy." A comma should go before the conjunction *and* in a list of three or more items. A comma after the next-to-last item in a series is called a serial comma.

15. B: What town did your parent's grow up in?
Error: apostrophe
An apostrophe is used to make something possessive, not plural. In this case, the proper word would be "parents".

16. B: The letter stated that my application had been denied, which was written on formal letterhead.
Error: misplaced modifier
The phrase "which was written on formal letterhead" describes the letter, which means that phrase should be placed immediately after the word "letter."

17. C: When my brother said he was going to the movies, I said I wanted to go to.
Error: wrong form of "to"
"To" is a direction. The proper form of the word here would be "too", meaning "also."

18. B: The movie was totally sold out; which stinks.
Error: semicolon
The semicolon between "out" and "which" is incorrect. A semicolon should be used only between two complete phrases. "Which stinks" is not a complete phrase.

19. D: No mistake.

20. B: Steve loved jogging, hiking, and loved to bike.
Error: parallelism

21. A: Blogging has become a very popular form of communication in the future.
Error: tense agreement
The sentence begins in the past with "has become" and then ends with "in the future". All tenses need to be consistent. The sentence should read, "Blogging will become a very popular form of communication in the future."

22. D: No mistake.

23. A: "A mile isn't very far to run." said Steve.
Error: period
A comma should be placed at the end of dialogue, before quotation marks. The sentence should read, "A mile isn't very far to run," said Steve.

24. B: Principal Walters and governor Jones had a debate on television.
Error: capitalization
The word "governor" should be capitalized when it is part of a name.

25. D: No mistake.

26. D: No mistake.

27. B: When Sue went to the mall and bought shoes she also bought a dress and some sandals.
Error: This is a run on sentence.
To be correct, the sentence would need to be broken up ("When Sue went to the mall, she bought shoes. She also bought a dress and some sandals.") or modified with a comma ("When Sue went to the mall and bought shoes, she also bought a dress and some sandals.")

28. A: Randall were very nervous on his wedding day.
Error: subject-verb agreement
Randall is one individual; therefore the singular form of the verb, "was", should be used rather than the plural form, "were".

29. C: Two wrongs don't not make a right.
Error: double negative
"Don't" is the contracted form of "do not." Saying "don't not" is the same as saying "do not not", which is a double negative.

30. B: I went to the store, but I forgot to buy bread
Error: punctuation
There is no period at the end of the sentence.

31. A: George gets tired very easily especially when he is doing hard work.
Error: comma
There should be a comma between "easily" and "especially".

32. D: No mistake.

33. A: I went to the hospital to talk to the doctor on Grant Street.
Error: misplaced modifier
The hospital is located on Grant Street, so that phrase should be placed directly after "hospital", making the sentence read, "I went to the hospital on Grant Street to talk to the doctor."

34. D: No mistake.

35. C
I always enjoyed reading, writing, and to sing a song.
Error: parallelism

- 144 -

All items in a list should be structured the same way. In this list, that means the final phrase should be "singing" to maintain the "-ing" structure.

36. B: Her favorite subject in school was english.
Error: capitalization
"English" is a proper noun and should be capitalized.

37. A: I love movies, and television, but I like reading better.
Error: comma
There is no need for a comma between "movies" and "television."

38. B: He will go to the game, but didn't stay long.
Error: agreement
"Will go to the game" is in the future. "Didn't stay long" is in the past. Both tenses need to be the same. The sentence should read either, "He went to the game, but didn't stay long." or "He will go to the game, but he will not stay long."

39. B: If you give the dog it's bone, it might stop begging for food.
Error: wrong word choice
"It's" is a contraction meaning "it is." The proper word in this sentence would be "its."

40. D: No mistake

41. B: "Lazie" should be spelled "lazy."

42. D: No mistake.

43. A: "Wreked" should be spelled "wrecked."
44. D: No mistake.

45. C: "Tecnician" should be spelled "technician."

46. A: "Aparpment" should be spelled "apartment."

47. C: "Overwait" should be spelled "overweight."

48. B: "Their" should be spelled "there."

49. D: No mistake.

50. C: "Accepted" should be spelled "expected."

51. B: The sentence "The iPad is the most popular of the new tablet computers" introduces the iPad, which is discussed further in sentence 3.

52. A: The sentence "His most famous novel is probably *The Adventures of Huckleberry Finn*" introduces the novel, which is the subject of the remainder of the paragraph.

53. A: Volleyball is a team sport that follows the verb "to play," whereas individual sports like yoga follow the verb "to do."

54. D: The word "every" is a singular noun and should be followed by a singular pronoun. In this case, the only singular pronoun is "her."

55. A: The subject of this sentence, "a team," is singular, so the verb also should be singular.

56. D: In the other sentences, the modifier is placed too far away from the word it modifies.

57. A: This sentence contains a number of parallel structures that must be treated consistently.

58. A: In this sentence, *whose* is the appropriate possessive pronoun to modify *opinion*.

59. B: Sentence 3, which is about the Yankees and their famous players, does not fit the overall topic of the Yankees and their World Series titles.

60. D: Sentence 5 relates a personal experience, which is off the topic of the controversial nature of climate change.

Quantitative Skills Explanations

1. D: Think of the numbers as they would be on a number line to place them in the correct order.

2. D: Rotational symmetry is defined as a figure that looks exactly the same after being rotated any amount. Answer choice D is the only example given that would stay the same if rotated

3. C: In this problem, if you do not know how to solve, try filling in the answer choices to see which one checks out. Many math problems may be solved by a guess and check method when you have a selection of answer choices.
$27 - x = -5$
$x = 32$

4. B: If you draw a vertical line down the center of the letter V, the two sides will be symmetrical.

5. D: To solve:
$8 \times 1 = 8$
$8 \times 2 = 16$
$8 \times 3 = 24$
$8 \times 4 = 32$
$8 \times 5 = 40$

6. A: Simplify the fraction by dividing both the numerator and the denominator by their greatest common factor. In this case, the greatest common factor is 11. When you do that, 44/99 becomes 4/9.

7. D: Find the common denominator for the two fractions so that you can compare them. You can use the common denominator of 45, as follows:
$2/5 = 18/45$
$4/9 = 20/45$
Look at the numerators: 18 and 20. The number halfway between them is 19, so the answer is 19/45

8. A: The fraction of ½ is the same as 50%. None of the other fractions are equal to that.

9. A: $250 \div 5 = 50$
All of the other divisors leave a remainder, as follows:
$250 \div 15 = 16$ r. 10
$250 \div 20 = 12$ r. 10
$250 \div 30 = 8$ r. 10

10. A: The mean, or average of the distribution can be computed by multiplying each grade by the number of students obtaining it, summing, and dividing by the total number of students. Here, $n = 4.2$. The median is the value for which an equal number of students have received higher or lower grades. Here, $p = 4$. The mode is the most frequently obtained grade, and here, $q = 3$.

11. B: Since there are equal numbers of each coin in the row, if two of one type are next to each other, two of the other type must also be next to each other someplace within the row, or else at

each end of the row. Since the two dimes take up one end of the row, the two pennies must be together.

12. A: The median of a set of numbers is one for which the set contains an equal number of greater and lesser values. Besides Z, there are 8 numbers in the set, so that 4 must be greater and 4 lesser than Z. The 4 smallest values are 5, 7, 9, and 12. The 4 largest are 16, 18, 23, and 44. So Z must fall between 12 and 16.

13. C: Find the common denominator of $3/8$ and $13/24$.
$3/8 \times 3/3 = 9/24$
$13/24 \times 1/1 = 13/24$
The value in the triangle must be greater than $9/24$ and less than $13/24$. Choice (C), $5/12$, when expressed as the equivalent fraction $10/24$, is correct.

14. D: Integers include all positive and negative whole numbers and the number zero. The product of three integers must be an integer, so you can eliminate any answer choice that is not a whole number: choices (A) and (C). The product of two even integers is even. The product of even and odd integers is even. The only even choice is 24.

15. D: Segment AD = 48. Because the length of CD is 2 times the length of AB, let $AB = x$ and let $CD = 2x$. Since $AB = BC$, let $BC = x$ also. The total length of $AD = AB + BC + CD = x + x + 2x = 4x = 48$. Thus, $x = 12$ and $BC + CD = x + 2x = 3x = 3 \times 12 = 36$.

16. D: .33 is equal to roughly $1/3$, so find which choice is NOT less (i.e. greater) than $1/3$. Since the "3" in the denominator of $1/3$ is a factor of the denominators of all the answer choices, you can compare the fractions with relative ease.

17. B: Double the number that is added to the previous number. So, 4+2=6,   6+4=10, 10+8=18, 18+16=34, and 34+32=66.

18. B: The equation for perimeter (P) = 2L + 2W. So, 600 = 2(250) + 2W. Solve f   or W: 600 – 500 = 2W. 100 = 2W. W = 50.

19. D: Multiplying a negative number by another negative number yields a positive number, in this case -2 x -10 = +20, which is the largest answer choice.

20. B: (0.25)X = 80. X = 80/0.25. X = 320.
21. A: The correct answer is B = 3A - 2.

22. D: (75 + 65 + 80 + 95 + 65)/5 = 76.

23. D: -10 is greater than -(-(-15)), which can also be written as -15.

24. B: T + C = 21. T = 3C + 1. If you solve for 21 – C = 3C + 1, you get 3C + C = 20. 4C = 20. C = 5.

25. A: 24/X = 60/100 = 3/5. 24 x 5 = 3X. 120 = 3X. X = 40.

26. B: A 20% increase in both sides gives dimensions of 24 and 36. To find the area, we multiply 24 x 36 and get 864 square inches.

27. D: Since the figure represents the number line, the distance from point A to point B will be the difference, *B-A*, which is $5 - (-6) = 11$. The distance from point B to point C will also be the difference, *C-B*, otherwise $8 - 5 = 3$. So the ratio *BC:AB* will be 3:11.

28. D: When a number is raised to a power, it is multiplied by itself as many times as the power indicates. For example, $2^3 = 2 \times 2 \times 2 = 8$. A number raised to the power of 0 is always equal to 1, so 6^0 is the smallest number shown. Similarly, for the other numbers: $9 = 9^1 = 9$; $10^1 = 10$; $4^2 = 4 \times 4 = 16$.

29. A: Let *D* represent Dorothy's age, and *S* her sister's. Since she is half her sister's age today, we have $D = \dfrac{S}{2}$, or $S = 2D$. In twenty years, her age will be $D + 20$ years, and her sister's age will be $S + 20$ years. At that time, Dorothy will be ¾ of her sister's age; therefore, $D + 20 = \dfrac{3 \times (S + 20)}{4}$.

Substituting 2*D* for *S* in this equation gives

$$D + 20 = \frac{3(2D + 20)}{4}$$

$$D + 20 = \frac{6D + 60}{4} \qquad \text{Use Distributive property and reduce.}$$

$$D + 20 = \frac{3}{2}D + 15$$

$$D + 20 = \frac{3D}{2} + 15$$

Gathering like terms:

$$20 - 15 = \frac{3D}{2} - D \text{ which is equivalent to } 5 = \frac{D}{2}.$$

Therefore, *D* = 10 years old. Dorothy is ten years old today, and her sister is twenty years old. In twenty years, Dorothy will be 30 years old, and her sister will be 40.

30. A: Lines 1 and 2 are parallel. If the parallel lines continued on into infinity, they would never cross. To *intersect* means that the lines cross. *Bisect* means that a line cuts another line or figure in two equal halves. To *correspond* means to match.

31. A: 30% of 50 is determined by multiplying 30/100 x 50. The answer is 15. Then, we need to find the number that 15 is 50% (or ½) of. This can be found by using the equation 15 = 1/2x. x = 30.

32. B: The average of 7 and x is 7 + x divided by 2. The average of 9, 4, and x is 9 + 4 + x divided by 3. (7+x)/2 = (9+4+x)/3. Simplify the problem and eliminate the denominators by multiplying the first side by 3 and the second side by 2. For the first equation, (21 + 3x)/6. For the second equation, (18 + 8 + 2x)/6. Since the denominators are the same, they can be eliminated, leaving 21 + 3x = 26 + 2x. Solving for x gets x = 26-21. x = 5.

33. D: This is a simple average problem. If x denotes Annie's score, 86+98+90+x, divided by 4 equals 92. To solve, multiply each side by 4 and add the known scores together to get 274 + x = 368. Subtract 274 from 368 to solve for x. x = 94.

34. B: One side of a square is 56cm. All of its sides are equal, and the perimeter is the sum of all sides.
Therefore, the perimeter equals 56cm+56cm+56cm+56cm
The perimeter is 224cm.

35. A: There are three fractions: 1/4, 1/8, and 1/2.
To answer the question, they have to be added. The common denominator is 8.
2/8 + 1/8 + 4/8 = 7/8
Among just the first three people, the dog is being taken care of 7/8 of the time.
Now, the time that is left over must be calculated.
Using the common denominator of 8, we know that 1 = 8/8
Therefore, to calculate the proportion of time the fourth person will have to care for the dog:
8/8 – 7/8 = 1/8

36. D
First, calculate 3% of 548 meters.
548 meters × 0.03 = 16.44 meters.
Then, add it to the original height.
548 meters + 16.44 meters = 564.44 meters
Rounding off, we get 564 meters.

37. D: Let x stand for the length and let y stand for the width of the rectangle. Then the area is expressed as the product xy. But if the length and width are doubled to 2x and 2y respectively, the area becomes $(2x)(2y)$ = $4xy$, which is 4 times as large as the original rectangle. "Four times as large" is equivalent to a 300 percent increase.

38. B: First calculate the difference 35 – 31 = 4. Then divide by the original price and multiply by 100 to find the percent increase: $(4 \div 31) \times 100$ = 12.9.

39. C: In answer A, $\frac{4}{5}$ of 80 is the same as 0.8 times 80, or 64. In answer B, 20% of 20 is the same as 0.2 times 20, or 4. In answer C, 7% of 1,400 is the same as 0.07 times 1,400, or 98. In answer D, 32 + 4 = 36.

40. A: A set of six numbers with an average of 4 must have a collective sum of 24. The two numbers that average 2 will add up to 4, so the remaining numbers must add up to 20. The average of these four numbers can be calculated: 20/4 = 5.

41. C: Prime numbers are those that are only evenly divisible by one and themselves.

42. C. There are 12 inches in a foot and 3 feet in a yard. Four and a half yards is equal to 162 inches. To determine the number of 3-inche segments, divide 162 by 3.

43. C: Since 4 is the same as 2^2, $4^6 = 2^{12}$. When dividing exponents with the same base, simply subtract the exponent in the denominator from the exponent in the numerator.

44. D: This problem can be solved with the following equation, in which x = the total capacity of the tank: $\frac{1}{2}x = \frac{1}{3}x + 3$.

45. C: The product is the result of multiplying two numbers.
The product of 13 x 7 = 91. Add 12 to get 103, Choice C.

46. A: The number must be evenly divisible by 3, 4, and 5 to be a multiple of all three numbers. Choice A is the correct answer.

47. B: The mode is the value of the term that occurs most. Of these terms, the number 14 occurs twice, so Choice B is the correct answer.

48. D: To increase a number by a given percent, take the percent of the original number and add it to the original number
65 x .33 = 21.45
Add the result to the original number:
21.45 + 65 = 86.45, Choice D.

49. C: Remember the order of operations when solving this equation. First, simplify all operations inside parentheses. Second, simplify any exponential expressions. Third, perform all multiplications and divisions as they occur in the problem from left to right. Fourth, perform all additions and subtractions as they occur in the problem from left to right:
2(7 + 8)2 – 12 (6 x 2) = 2(15) 2 – 12(12)
= 2(225) – 12(12)
= 450 – 144 = 306, Choice C.

50. B: Compare each place value of every number to determine the largest number. Since there are all zeros in the ones place, move to the tenths place. Two tenths is larger than the other numbers, Choice B.

51. D: To change this number from scientific notation to standard notation, move the decimal point to the right six places:
2.34×10^6 = 2,340,000, Choice D.

52. A: To subtract these two integers, change the subtraction sign to addition, then change the sign of the number being subtracted to its opposite:
-9 - (-8) = -9 + 8 = -1, Choice A.

Mathematics Explanations

1. D: The fraction of those playing drums plus the fraction of those playing a brass instrument must total 1. So the number that play drums is pn, and the number playing brass must be $(1-p)n$.

A. $pn-1$ is one less than the number playing drums.
B. $p(n-1)$ applies the proportion to fewer than the total number of musicians.
C. $(p-1)n$ results in a negative number (since p must be less than 1).

2. D: An easy way to do this is to remember that for a number to be divisible by 3, the sum of the digits must be divisible by 3. Thus, for 555, 5+5+5=15, and 15/3 = 5. 555/3 = 185

A. 2+0+1+8 = 11, which is not divisible by 3.
B. 4+6 = 10, which is not divisible by 3.
C. 8+9+1+2=20, which is not divisible by 3.

3. D: Distance is the product of velocity and time, and (5×10^6) x $2 \times 10^{-4} = (10 \times 10^6 \times 10^{-4}) =$ $10^3 = 1000$.

A. $50 \neq (5 \times 10^6)$ x 2×10^{-4}
B. $25 \neq (5 \times 10^6)$ x 2×10^{-4}
C. $100 \neq (5 \times 10^6)$ x 2×10^{-4}

4. B: 25% off is equivalent to $25 \times \dfrac{\$138}{100} = \$34.50$, so the sale price becomes \$138 - \$34.50 = \$103.50.

A. \$67 $\neq$ \$103.50
C. \$34.50 is the amount of the reduction, not the final price.
D. \$113 $\neq$ \$103.50

5. C: The expression 2^{-3} is equivalent to $\dfrac{1}{2^3}$, and since $2^3 = 8$, it is equivalent to 1/8.

A. $\dfrac{1}{4} = 2^{-2}$

B. $\dfrac{1}{12} \neq \dfrac{1}{8}$

D. $\dfrac{1}{16} = 2^{-4}$

6. C: The surface of a cube is obtained by multiplying the area of each face by 6, since there are 6 faces. The area of each face is the square of the length of one edge. Therefore $A = 6 \times 3^2 = 6 \times 9 = 54$.

7. A: The area A of a circle is given by $A = \pi \times r^2$, where r is the radius. Since π is approximately 3.14, we can solve for $r = \sqrt{\dfrac{A}{\pi}} = \sqrt{\dfrac{314}{3.14}} = \sqrt{100} = 10$. Now, the diameter d is twice the radius, or $d = 2 \times 10 = 20$.

B. 10 is the value of the radius, not the diameter.

8. D: Inspection of the data shows that the distance traveled by the car during any 1-unit interval (velocity) is 20 units. However, the first data point shows that the car is 50 units from the point of origin at time 2, so it had a 10-unit head start before time measurement began.

Answers A-C only fit the data at single points. They do not fit the whole set.

9. A: The perimeter of a circle is given by $2\pi r$, where r is the radius. We solve for $r = \dfrac{35}{2\pi} = 5.57$, and double this value to obtain the diameter $d = 11.14$ feet.

Since this value is unique, all the other answers are incorrect. Answer C is the radius, not the diameter.

10. D: There are two ways to solve this problem: either convert meters to centimeters and then use the conversion factor in the table to convert centimeters to inches, or else use the table to convert meters to yards, and then convert to inches.

In the first instance, recall that there are 100 centimeters in a meter (*centi* means "hundredth"). Therefore $19 \text{ m} = 1900 \text{ cm} = \left(\dfrac{1900}{2.54}\right) = 748$ inches.

In the second instance, recall that there are 36 inches in a yard, therefore $19 \text{ m} = 19 \times 1.094 = 20.786 \text{ yd} = 20.786 \times 36 = 748$ inches.

Proportions are commonly used for conversions. After converting meters to centimeters set up proportions to solve for an unknown variable, x.

$\dfrac{900 \text{ cm}}{x \text{ in}} = \dfrac{2.54 \text{ cm}}{1 \text{ in}}$ Cross multiply.

$900 = 2.54x$ Divide each side by 2.54 to solve for x.

$x = 748$

11. B: The inequality specifies that the difference between L and 15 inches must be less or equal to 0.01. For choice B, $| 14.99 - 15 | = | -0.01 | = 0.01$, which is equal to the specified tolerance and therefore meets the condition.

$|14.9 - 15| = | -0.1 | = 0.1$ which is greater than 0.01.
and D. are both longer than the length L and therefore not the minimum length.
14.991 is within the acceptable tolerance range, but is longer than 14.99.

12. D: The product of x and $\dfrac{1}{x}$ is $\dfrac{1}{x} \times x = \dfrac{x}{x} = 1$. The expression x^{-1} is equivalent to $\dfrac{1}{x}$. Thus, both B and C are correct.

    A. $(x-1) \times x = x^2 - x \neq 1$

13. D: Each term of each expression in parentheses must be multiplied by each term in the other. Thus for E, $(x+3)(3x-5) = 3x^2 + 9x - 5x - 15 = 3x^2 + 4x - 15$

    A. $(x-3)(x+5) = x^2 - 3x + 5x - 15 = x^2 + 2x - 15 \neq 3x^2 + 4x - 15$

    B. $(x+5)(3+x^2) = 3x + 15 + x^3 + 5x^2 \neq 3x^2 + 4x - 15$

    C. $x(3x + 4 - 15) = 3x^2 + 4x - 15x = 3x^2 - 11x \neq 3x^2 + 4x - 15$

14. B: First determine the proportion of students in Grade 5. Since the total number of students is 180, this proportion is $\dfrac{36}{180} = 0.2$, or 20%. Then determine the same proportion of the total prizes, which is 20% of twenty, or $0.2 \times 20 = 4$.

    A. $5 \neq 0.2 \times 20$

    C. $7 \neq 0.2 \times 20$

    D. $3 \neq 0.2 \times 20$

15. A: From the starting expression, compute:

$$3\left(\frac{6x-3}{3}\right) - 3(9x+9) = 3(2x-1) - 27x - 27 = 6x - 3 - 27x - 27 = -21x - 30 = -3(7x+10)$$

    B. $-3x + 6 \neq 3\left(\dfrac{6x-3}{3}\right) - 3(9x+9)$

    C. $(x+3)(x-3) = x^2 + 3x - 3x - 9 = x^2 - 9 \neq 3\left(\dfrac{6x-3}{3}\right) - 3(9x+9)$

    D. $3x^2 - 9 \neq 3\left(\dfrac{6x-3}{3}\right) - 3(9x+9)$

16. B: Compute as follows: $(3 - 2 \times 2)^2 = (3-4)^2 = (-1)^2 = 1$.

    C is incorrect since $4 \neq 2$.

All other answers are incorrect since they are negative, and the squared expression must be greater than 0.

17. C: Evaluate as follows:

$$(3x^{-2})^3 = 3^3 \times (x^{-2})^3 = 27 \times (\frac{1}{x^2})^3 = 27 \times \frac{1}{x^8} = 27x^{-8}$$

A. $9x^{-6} \neq 27x^{-8}$
B. $9x^{-8} \neq 27x^{-8}$
D. $27x^{-4} \neq 27x^{-8}$

18. B: The lowest score, 68, is eliminated. The average of the remaining four grades is

$$Avg = \frac{75 + 88 + 86 + 90}{4} = 84.75$$

Rounding up to the nearest integer gives a final grade of 85. Since this value is unique, all the other answers are incorrect.

19. B: To calculate S, calculate the discount and subtract it from the original price, p. The discount is 33% of p, or $0.33p$. Thus, $S = p - 0.33p$.

A. $S = p - 0.33 \neq$ p-0.33p
C. $S = 0.33p \neq$ p-0.33p
D. $S = 0.33(1-p) \neq$ p-0.33p

20. C: The volume of a right circular cylinder is equal to its height multiplied by the area of its base, A. Since the base is circular, $A = \pi R^2$, where R, the radius, is half the diameter, or 30 feet. Therefore,

$$V = H \times \pi R^2$$

Solving for H,

$$H = \frac{V}{\pi R^2} = \frac{1,000,000}{\pi \times 30^2} = \frac{1,000,000}{\pi \times 900} \approx 353.7\,\text{ft}$$

A and B are both greater than 355, so they do not represent the minimum acceptable height. D is too low to hold the required volume.

21. C: Rearranging the equation gives
$3(x+4)=15(x-5)$, which is equivalent to
$15x-3x=12+75$, or
$12x=87$, and solving for x,
$$x=\frac{87}{12}=\frac{29}{4}.$$

Since this value is unique, all the other answers are incorrect.

22. B: The median is the value in a group of numbers that separates the upper half from the lower half, so that there are an equal number of values above and below it. In this distribution, there are two values greater than 116, and two values below it.
A. is the mean, or average of the distribution, not the median.
C. is the most common value, or mode of the distribution, not the median.
D is simply a value within the range of the distribution. It is not the median.

23. D: The product $(a)(a)(a)(a)(a)$ is defined as a to the fifth power.
A. $5a = 5 \times a \ne a^5$
B. $a^{-5} = \dfrac{1}{a^5} \ne a^5$
C. $a^{\frac{1}{5}} = \sqrt[5]{a} \ne a^5$

24. A: Rearranging the equation gives $x^2 = -1$. However, the square of a real number cannot yield a negative result, so no real number solutions exist for the equation.

Answers B-D are incorrect, since it has been shown that there are no real number solutions.

25. A: Begin by determining the total cost of the onions and carrots, since these prices are given. This will equal (2 x $3.69) + (3 x $4.29) = $20.25. Next, this sum is subtracted from the total cost of the vegetables to determine the cost of the mushrooms: $24.15 - $20.25 = $3.90. Finally, the cost of the mushrooms is divided by the quantity (lbs) to determine the cost per pound:
$$\text{Cost per lb} = \frac{\$3.90}{1.5} = \$2.60$$

26. D. The perimeter (P) of the quadrilateral is simply the sum of its sides, or
$P = m + (m+2) + (m+3) + 2m$
Combine like terms by adding the variables (m terms) together and then adding the constants resulting in:
$P = 5m + 5$
In this application, it appears that some of the variables do not have a number in front of them; however, the absence of a coefficient indicates multiplication by 1 hence $m = 1m$, $x = 1x$, and so on.

- 156 -

27. C: First determine the total distance of the round trip. This is twice the 45 miles of the one-way trip to work in the morning, which equals 90 miles. Then, determine the total amount of time Elijah spent on his round trip by converting his travel times into minutes. One hour and ten minutes equals 70 minutes, and one and a half hours equal 90 minutes. Elijah's total travel time was 70 + 90 = 160 minutes. Elijah's average speed can now be determined in miles per minute:

$$\text{Speed} = \frac{90 \text{ miles}}{160 \text{ min}} = 0.5625 \text{ miles per minute}$$

Finally, to convert this average speed into miles per hour, multiply by 60, since there are 60 minutes in an hour:
Avg speed (mph) = 60 x 0.5625 = 33.75 miles per hour

28. D: Begin as you would a regular equation.

$$4x - 12 > 4$$

$$+12 \quad +12 \qquad\qquad \text{Add 12 to each side}$$

$$\frac{4x}{4} < \frac{16}{4} \qquad\qquad \text{Divide each side by 4}$$

Note that the inequality does not change because the division was by a *positive* 4.
Since x must be less than 4, and not equal to it (< not ≤), the answer A is incorrect the solution does not include 4. Only answer D satisfies the condition that it be less than 4.

29. D: First, compute the value enclosed by the parentheses, $3b + 5 = 3 \times 7 + 5 = 26$. Next, compute $4a$ = -24. Note that a is negative, so that this product is negative as well. The product $4a(3b + 5)$ will therefore be negative as well, and equals -624. Finally, add the value of $2b$, or 2 x 7 =14, to -624, to get the final answer $624 + 14 = -610$.
Substitute the given values for the variables into the expression
4·-**6** (3 · **7** +5) + 2· **7**
Using order of operations, compute the expression in the parentheses first.
Remember that first you must multiply 3 by 7, then add 5 in order to follow order of operations
=4·-**6** (21 +5) + 2· **7**   Next add the values in the parenthesis.
= 4·-**6** (26) + 2· **7**   Simplify by multiplying the numbers outside the parenthesis.
=-24(26) +14   Multiply -24 by 26
=-624 +14   Add.
=-610

30. C: Define the variable t as the elapsed time (in hours) from the time the first airplane takes off. Then at any time the distance traveled by the first plane is $d_1 = 250t$. The second plane takes off 30 minutes later, so at any time the distance that it has traveled is: $d_2 = 280(t - 30)$. This plane will overtake the first when the two distances are equal, that is when $d_1 = d_2$, or when $250t = 280(t - 30)$. First use the distributive property to solve for t: $250t = 280t - 8400$.
Next, add 8400 to each side of the equation: $250t + 8400 = 280t$.
Next, subtract $250t$ from each side of the equation: $8400 = 30t$.
Next, divide both sides by 30: 280 = t.
This gives the value of t in minutes. Convert to hours by dividing 280 by 60 minutes per hour, which yields an elapsed time of 4 hours and 40 minutes (remember to multiply decimal (.66...) by 60 in order to convert decimal into minutes (40 min). Since the first plane left at 2 PM, 4 hours and 40 minutes later is 6:40 PM.

31. D: In order to multiply two powers that have the same base, add their exponents. Therefore, $x^3 x^5 = x^{3+5} = x^8$.

Also note that x³=x·x·x; therefore the expression equals x·x·x · x·x·x·x·x

32. B: A proportion such as this can be solved by taking the cross product of the numerators and denominators from either side.

$$\frac{12}{x} = \frac{30}{6}$$ Take the cross product by cross multiplication

$30x = 6 \times 12$ Multiply 6 by 12

$30x = 72$ Divide each side by 30.

$x = 2.4$

33. A: This equation represents a linear relationship that has a slope of 3.60 and passes through the origin. The table indicates that for each hour of rental, the cost increases by $3.60. This corresponds to the slope of the equation. Of course, if the bicycle is not rented at all (0 hours) there will be no charge ($0). If plotted on the Cartesian plane, the line would have a y intercept of 0. Relationship *A* is the only one that satisfies these criteria.

34. D: Rafael's profit on each computer is given by the difference between the price he pays and the price he charges his customer, or $800-$450. If he sells *n* computers in a month, his total profit will be *n* times this difference, or $n(800-450)$. However, it is necessary to subtract his fixed costs of $3000 from this to compute his final profit per month.

35. D: When a number is raised to a power, it is multiplied by itself as many times as the power indicates. For example, $2^3 = 2 \times 2 \times 2 = 8$. A number raised to the power of 0 is always equal to 1, so 6^0 is the smallest number shown. Similarly, for the other numbers: $9 = 9^1 = 9$; $10^1 = 10$; $4^2 = 4 \times 4 = 16$.

36. D: It is not necessary to use the circle formula to solve the problem. Rather, note that 50 km/hr corresponds to 50,000 meters per hour. We are given the car's revolutions per minute and the answer must be represented as meters; therefore, the speed must be converted to meters per minute. This corresponds to a speed of $\frac{50,000}{60}$ meters per minute, as there are 60 minutes in an hour. In any given minute the car travels ($\frac{50,000}{60}$ meters/min), the tires rotate 500 times around, hence 500 times its circumference. This corresponds to $\frac{50,000}{60 \times 500} = \frac{10}{6}$ meters per revolution, which is the circumference of the tire.

37. A: Compute the product using the FOIL method, in which the *F*irst term, then the *O*uter terms, the *I*nner terms, and finally the *L*ast terms are figured in sequence of multiplication. As a result, $(a+b)(a-b) = a^2 + ba - ab - b^2$. Since *ab* is equal to *ba*, the middle terms cancel each other which leaves $a^2 - b^2$.

38. D: The area of the circle is πr² while the circumference is 2πr. Taking the ratio of these two expressions and reducing gives: $Ratio = \frac{\pi r^2}{2\pi r} = \frac{r}{2}$

39. A: Complementary angles are two angles that equal 90° when added together.

40. C: $29 + r = 420$
$29 + r - 29 = 420 - 29$
$r = 391$

41. C: To solve, find the sum. $35\% + 4\% = 39\%$

42. C: Electronics sales $= x$
$x = 35 + (-2) + (-1) + (+6) + (-1) + (+2)$
$x = (35 + 6 + 2) + (-2 + (-1) + (-1))$
$x = (43) + (-4)$
$x = 39$

43. C: Solve as follows:
$5/8 = x/100$
$5 \cdot 100 \div 8 = x$
$x = 62.5$

44. B: These are supplementary angles. That means that the two angles will add up to a total of 180°, which is the angle of a straight line. To solve, subtract as follows:
$b = 180° - 120°$
$b = 60°$

45. B: Add to solve. The height of the window from the floor is not needed in this equation. It is extra information. You only need to add the heights of the two bookcases. Change the fractions so that they have a common denominator. After you add, simply the fraction.
$14\frac{1}{2} + 8\frac{3}{4}$
$= 14\,2/4 + 8\frac{3}{4}$
$= 22\,5/4$
$= 23\frac{1}{4}$

46. C: 10% of $1000 = $100
$1000 + $100 = $1100
10% of $1100 = $110
$1100 - $110 = $990

47. B: $y = x + 5$, and you were told that $x = -3$. Fill in the missing information for x, then solve.
$y = (-3) + 5$
$y = 2$

48. D: You would write the negative square root of 100 as follows:
$-\sqrt{100}$

49. A: Add the numbers with x together, as follows: $5x + 4x = 9x$
Add the y numbers, as follows: $-2y + y = -y$
Put the x and y numbers back into the same equation: $9x - y$.

50. B: To solve, line up the like terms, as follows:

$$3x^2 + x + 3$$
$$+8x^2 + 5x + 16$$
$$\overline{11x^2 + 6x + 19}$$

51. C: A straight line is 180°. Subtract to solve: 180° - 45° = 135°

52. B: The average rate of cooling is: (86º - 38º) / 9 hrs; 48º / 9 = 5.33º F per hour.

53. B: Double the number that is added to the previous number. So, 4+2=6, 6+4=10, 10+8=18, 18+16=34, and 34+32=66.

54. A: $(x^2)^3 = x^{(2 \times 3)} = x^6$; $(y^2)^5 = y^{(2 \times 5)} = y^{10}$; $(y^4)^3 = y^{(4 \times 3)} = y^{12}$; $y^{10} \cdot y^{12} = y^{(10+12)} = y^{22}$.

55. B: $(x^2)^5 y^6 z^2 / x^4 (y^3)^4 z^2 = x^{(2 \times 5)} - x^4 = x^{10} - x^4 = x^6$; $y^6 - y^{(3 \times 4)} = y^6 - y^{12} = y^{-6}$; $z^2 - z^2 = z^0$ or 0; so the answer is: $x^6 y^{-6}$.

56. D: 1 gallon = 128 ounces, so 8 x 128 = 1,024 ounces for 8 gallons. ½ = 64 gallons, and ¼ = 32 gallons, so 64 + 32 = 96 ounces to fill the ¾ gallons; the total ounces required is 1,024 + 96 = 1,120 ounces.

57. A: Using the Pythagorean theorem: $25^2 + 35^2 = c^2$. 625 + 1225 = c^2. c = sqrt 1850 = 43.01.

58. A: ½ / 15 = 4 3/5 / X; ½ X = 15 x 23/5. ½ X = 69. X = 69 x 2 = 138.

59. A: $V = \pi r^2 h$. V = 3.14 x (3^2) x 12. 3.14 x 9 x 12 = 339.12.

60. B: The equation for perimeter (P) = 2L + 2W. So, 600 = 2(250) + 2W. Solve for W: 600 – 500 = 2W. 100 = 2W. W = 50.

61. C: (0.45 + 0.0 + 0.75 + 1.20 + 1.1 + 0.2 + 0.0) / 7 = 0.53.

62. A: 55 x 7/100 = 55 x .07 = 3.85.

63. B: He gets paid $12.00/hr for the first 40 hrs: 12 x 40 = $480. For time-and-a-half: 5 x 1.5 = 7.5. 7.5 x 12 = $90. So, 480 + 90 = $570.

64. D: 1 yard = 3 feet. (5 1/3 yards / X) x (3 feet/1 yard) = 16/3 x 3 = 48/3. X = 16.